PULSES OF THE DIVINE HEART

Kalu Onwuka

Granada Publishers

Los Angeles, California

Pulses of the Divine Heart

Copyright ©2014 by Kalu Onwuka

Published in Los Angeles, California by Granada Publishers. Granada Publishers is wholly owned by the Granada Publishing Company, Los Angeles, California.

Granada Publishing titles may be purchased in bulk for educational, fundraising or sales promotional use. For more information please e-mail **sales@granadapublishing.com**

All rights reserved. No part of this publication may be reproduced, stored in a retrieval system or transmitted in any form or by any means-electronic, mechanical, digital, photocopy, recording or any other-except for brief quotations in printed reviews, without the written permission of the copyright owner.

Library of Congress Control Number

Pulses of the Divine Heart/ Kalu Onwuka

LCCN: 2014911259

ISBN: 978-0-9900203-5-6

ISBN: 0990020355

Printed in the United States

DEDICATION

I will like to dedicate this book, *Pulses of the Divine Heart* which is the second volume of *Ruminations on the Golden Strand* series, to all those who share the gifts of light and love everywhere in the world either in formal or informal settings. Yours is not an easy task for truth is very hard to tell and often falls on deaf ears in a world where the sweet and easy has become the norm. The world may or may not acclaim you but Heaven's promise is never to forget or forsake such as you that labor to keep the gate against the onslaught of darkness.

ACKNOWLEDGMENTS

As always, I will first like to acknowledge Christ Jesus as the Lord of my life. He is my muse and I write through his light. Also, I will like to acknowledge that it is not possible to see through an undertaking such as *Ruminations of the Golden Strand* series without the loyal support of family, friends and well-wishers. You have all been there from the beginning on through to the publication process. I will like to acknowledge all your assistance for you continue to give me cause to hope for the best in mankind. It is such goodness that you show that will help transform the world from what is today to the better that It can be in the future.

CONTENTS

Dedication		iii
Acknowledgments		iv
Introduction		v
Chapter 1	Walking in Light	1
Chapter 2	In the Footsteps and Heartbeat	11
Chapter 3	A Universal Language	21
Chapter 4	The Ultimate Victory	31
Chapter 5	Standing Firm	41
Chapter 6	Giving Back in Kind	49
Chapter 7	Under Sunshine of Love	61
Chapter 8	In Divine Immunity	73
Chapter 9	In Glorious Liberty	83
Chapter 10	Perfection in the Sum	93
Chapter 11	A Cleft in the Rock	105

CONTENTS

Chapter 12	Borne of the Good Tree	115
Chapter 13	The Emblem of Hope	125
Chapter 14	The Revitalized Life	137
Chapter 15	On the Road of Hope	149
Chapter 16	From Seed to Tree	159
Chapter 17	Under Divine Illumination	169
Chapter 18	Contentment with Godliness	179
Chapter 19	An Ordained Purpose	191
Chapter 20	Bond of Love	199
Chapter 21	Stars of Heaven	207
Chapter 22	The Walk of Fame	215

INTRODUCTION

This book titled *Pulses of the Divine Heart* is the second volume in the *Ruminations on the Golden Strand* series. The series encapsulate the author's experiences during his faith-walk and ultimate spiritual transformation in following after the footsteps of Christ Jesus. There are also numerous insights and observations drawn from real life experiences that help frame the truth contained herein in a way that the perceptive reader will find to be very informative and of invaluable assistance for spiritual transformation.

The book begins by highlighting the fact that the gift of perception is needed to be faithful on the path to spiritual transformation as the walk is not by sight but by faith. The journey truly begins when the seeker starts to 'see' through the darkness that masks so much in the world today for that is where the enemy of light lurks. The ability to see in this wise is the gift of perception. It is much needed for victorious living but he that desires it must embrace and remain obedient to Truth. The teachings of Christ Jesus embody Truth that enables perception and leads to spiritual maturity so that one no longer knows in part but in full about the important in life.

He that no longer knows in part but in full has been bestowed with the wisdom that avails mankind knowledge

Introduction

from beyond the limits of the flesh. He that is privy to such knowledge has received the 'vision of the eagle' for he now has the platform to know from a divine perspective. He can see the true picture concealed within things so as to sort out the important in life and not bother with the unimportant. He has become an exalted soul given to soar in spirit to the domain of the life bearing rain clouds. Most men, including those who profess to walk in the footsteps of Christ Jesus, trudge along close to the valley spiritually. They traverse the well-beaten and familiar tracks of the worldly. All who are enamored with worldliness will never grow to full maturity but remain spiritual dwarfs not able to be exalted for lack of vision.

The realm of the exalted or the kingdom of God is realized when one has fully grown in spirit to be in communion with the Divine. Living in the kingdom of God is the realm where mankind can have a foretaste of divine glory on earth. Such a way of life is definitely not today's norm but it will be the given for the new earth to come. It demands a very short leash on the flesh so that the spirit can have full rein to abound to the utmost. God is revealing so much these days to those who have come to full spiritual maturity in Christ. Indeed this is the season when many have come into true knowledge as stars of Heaven ordained to fill the night sky. The stars of Heaven are the exalted souls that can understand veiled truth and divine mysteries. Such ones have been given spiritual sight so that they can understand the divine mind for the benefit of their short sighted fellows. They are the sons of light prepared and positioned by God all over the world. They can foretell things to come so that those willing to embrace Truth can come into the safety of God's ark with them. Theirs is a noble calling that is not often appreciated in today's world but to God's glory many have come to glimpse divine light through the sons.

There is always a spiritual choke that every believer has to contend with. The spiritual choke is borne of the flesh. It is a major hindrance for the unbeliever and a cause for infirmity of spirit for the unwary believer. He that has doubt cannot begin to perceive and he that has an infirm spirit cannot be counted on to fight for God when it matters. The infirm believer may labor mightily but he will not reap much for he has set his faith to naught. The spiritual choke is the juggernaut of faith life. There is always a season when the believer is confronted with a decisive choice of who or what to lay down one's life for. It is really a choice between yielding to God and thereby life or death by yielding to the juggernaut. He that chooses to bow down to God is availed new life but he that bows to juggernaut becomes bound to the earthen.

The love that leads the faithful believer to lay down his life for God and the benefit of humanity is Charity. It is the sacrifice of inestimable value made so that others can be afforded the chance to be reconciled with and come into knowledge of the Heavenly Father. It is the hallmark

Introduction

of those who are fully matured and exalted in spirit that charity governs all their actions. By the same token, the Heavenly Father will always love such beyond measure that live by charity and faithful obedience in Christ.

No one starts on the path of spiritual transformation full of faith. Faith is like a seed that first has to be planted and cared for so as to grow and become strong. It takes some time to learn to fly on the wings of faith. It takes some time to master how to walk in the light of truth and love so as to realize the fullness of the riches of God through Christ. It takes some time to un-wrap the burial bandages of Lazarus and step out in strong faith in the spirit of the reborn in light. Strong faith is borne of long suffering patience and total trust in God. It comes with great vision and is divinely availed to the fully matured in spirit.

Everyone who has matured in spirit to be availed strong faith and great vision is given to live a spirit-led life that does not seek a stage or platform to find fulfillment. It is life lived in voluntary humility so that the spirit can remain firm to always have sway over the flesh at all times. Such an exalted soul does his work through Christ effacingly and not for public adulation so that God can have the glory. All who labor in this wise are those on whom the eye of the Heavenly Father rests at all times. Such twinkle in spirit as stars of Heaven and represent some of the Heavenly Father's infinite eyes by which he looks through the earth. Each star that twinkles in this way is a beacon given to shine so many others can glimpse the Divine.

Introduction

Truth is the element that bonds every faithful servant with the Divine. Christ is revealed in those who speak and love Truth regardless of cost. The lover of Truth already lives in accordance with the golden rule for he will not cut corners or take short cuts in his dealings with others. He that lives by Truth will have no iniquity or wickedness found in him. Rather he will travel on the path of righteousness and have no difficulty with all that God expects of mankind. Truth is the language spoken by all that live in glorious liberty for only that can set the spirit free to soar to the exalted realm. On the hand, he that hates Truth will forever remain bound to the earthy to lust after the material and transient.

On a cautionary note, it must be strongly emphasized that mankind is overly enamored with earthly materials. He is not able to understand that man reaps as he sows. He that sows in the material reaps corruption but he that sows in the spirit reaps life. The lust for material things leads mankind to cut corners, seek short cuts and compromise Truth. The lust for material things keeps the soul in bondage and leads the unwary to spiritual demise. The soul that is in bondage wallows in the miry clay of the earth and is unable to rise heavenward for lack of life in the spirit. Such will remain listless and hunger forever but will not find fulfillment in life. God is the source of both the fulfilling and of life itself. Therefore mankind must first be reconciled in spirit with the Divine in order to find such. Man's earthly sojourn becomes meaningless if he is unable to awake in spirit to reconcile with God and thereby find fulfillment in new life before his time expires.

The believer that is matured in spirit can ask and receive as he wishes from the Heavenly Father for goodness and mercy attends him. The matured in Christ duly receives in mercy from the Heavenly Father but is called to pass it forward in grace to whoever is willing to receive. Grace covers the believer in his spiritual journey through the infant days on to full maturity in Christ. For that reason, grace is foundational as well as all-encompassing in God's kingdom. It originates from a Divine impetus to course through time across the branches and up the boughs of the family tree of the righteous from those who have gone before to reach the believer just starting today.

No one can be counted to be fully matured in Christ until he has borne a spiritual offspring in the way of faith. Everyone must bear a child in the way of Christ to be deemed worthy before God. There are only a few things in man's spiritual experience that can compare to the fulfillment of bearing a child in the kingdom way as a spiritual father. It is an occasion of joy both in Heaven above and on earth below when that happens. He that has nurtured another in the way of Christ to help bring him into the light of God is his spiritual father. Both are linked in spirit by the cord of love to enter into that mystical bond through which divine blessing flows.

The mystical bond borne through sacrificial love for the

enlightenment of another through Christ is the motivation that showcases and validates the awesome power of God for man's benefit. The goodness and mercy that follow the father also reaches the son that walks in the shadow of his spiritual father. The bond of the father and son is the cradle of regeneration in that all which wisdom has bestowed on the father is passed on to the son in the light of Truth with love. The spiritual linkage between fathers and sons is such that there is no end but always a new beginning. It is the saga of the good fight fought and won, the race finished in victory, the triumph of light over darkness and the victory of life over death when the baton of the noble in spirit is passed on to the worthy receiver.

A new man remade in the Divine image of Christ always comes alive in due time when the baton of life is passed on to a worthy receiver. The man of the old nature is earthy and weighty. His destiny is death but the man of the new nature is starry and light. His destiny on the other hand is life forever. He that has become transformed in his inner man to the starry and light has become spiritually buoyant. No longer will he be bound to the earthy for he has overcome the world and can readily soar in spirit.

The spirit is willing to serve God long before the flesh becomes conditioned to do so. There is a reconfiguring of mind and body that takes place as the believer commits to serve God fully. Such a committed one will begin to discard many things of his old nature. In effect, he has begun to shed the 'weight' of the world so that his life can be streamlined to be more effective in his service to God and humanity. The streamlined life is a very productive one. Such a life is able to do more with less than he could in the past for he has begun to experience the redeeming power of God to add value to things, people and situations to make them better.

Often in his spiritual walk, mankind often dwells on what he can get from God instead of just keeping fellowship with him. God is not going anywhere. He is eternal and faithful in his promises. Rather the truly faithful seek to know how God can use them for his divine purposes. It is by fellowship or just being there with God that divine blessings abound for mankind. Keeping faith always is the only way for the believer to hear words of commendation from the Heavenly Father when his earthly walk is done.

The believer that is worthy of Divine commendation is one that is transformed in a Divine image. The seeker has to be willing to pass through the heart of the cross so as to be transformed in a Divine image. The heart of the cross represents the crossover point from the temporal into the eternal. The heart of the cross is where the world casts off the believer. The heart of the cross is where the believer has been abandoned by friends, family and others on account of his uncompromising love for God. It is a place where the believer is grossly misunderstood, derided and mocked for the most part. The heart of the cross is the crucible where the crucial choice between immortality and mortality is made. It is through the heart of the cross that the faithful is led into the congregation of the mighty in spirit who stand before God on behalf of other men.

The heart of the cross is the figurative eye of the needle. For mankind to be exalted in spirit, he must pass through this figurative eye of the needle. It takes the crucifixion suffered at the hands of the worldly to streamline the body and mind so that the spirit can pass through the eye of the needle to ascend to the exalted realm. He that can ascend in this wise becomes a son of God or a 'Christ-Man' with the ability to commute between heaven and earth in spirit. Such will be privy to the will of God and guided in spirit to serve the Divine purposes on earth.

The truly faithful seek greater understanding and knowledge. When greater understanding is followed with obedient living, a brighter divine illumination dawns in the life of the believer. He that is under greater illumination will twinkle as a star of hope by which others on earth may find their way. Such is an eternal star that will never grow dim or disappear as long as he remains a source of enlightenment for others to follow in the way of Christ. He that is faithful in this wise, will always draw from the well of divine wisdom and be attended well by Providence.

Lack of thankfulness to God for the gifts availed to mankind is the reason why many are not able to come into knowledge of the Divine. He that is unthankful for what he has received will become a malcontent in spirit who will lack the peace within that leads mankind into the greater and higher. Contentment of soul with due thankfulness for life's gifts leads to godliness and much gain. On the other hand, the malcontent in spirit will never know the full riches of the Divine but will always have lack in his soul. Sadly, it is such lack of contentment that defines the earthly existence for many and drives the selfishness that is so common these days.

Contentment of soul is a good indication of one's spiritual maturity. The fully matured in spirit will belong in the congregation of those being perfected in light and love. This congregation is a spiritual beehive that pulsates with the Divine urge. All congregants of this living church of Christ work towards the common goal of bringing the way of Heaven down to earth so as to evoke the new golden age of humanity. All who are joined up with the Divine in this mission have left ample room in life for the things that pertain to godliness and very little for life's clutters. Life's clutters often possess the soul to bring cloudiness to the mind. In the absence of cloudiness of mind, there is a definite certainty and clarity of purpose that leads mankind to seek after the heavenly. The mind that is set after Heaven hungers for a glorious dawn in which darkness ceases to exist among humanity. It is only in glorious dawn that orderliness returns to man's life, confusion recedes and focus is sharpened. It is only when certainty and clarity of purpose reigns in the soul that the spirit can be free to ascend heavenwards.

Introduction

At the end of the day, life on earth is but a grand performance aimed for the acclaim of Heaven. The star lit night is the silver screen and canvas that reflects the handiworks of those who have served God faithfully in twinkling majesty. Each star is an emblem of the son who has performed his role on earth masterfully so that his work is held up in immortal display for mortals to gaze at. Indeed it is only when the glory of God is shed on mankind that his handiwork is immortalized above. Everyone that faithfully lives by Truth is cast for a suitable role in life's grand performance. There are pre-destined and different roles to play in accordance with Divine will. All who have been cast for a part must follow the script and perform their roles with honor. The role performed well is the life lived in the light of Truth and love that serves humanity in goodness. The audience is the heavenly host that judges and records all of mankind's performances in the book of life where all who are worthy of honor are duly credited.

Finally, this book is not written to be a substitute for the Holy Bible but to help amplify its message of love and hope. In that light, I pray that the truth contained within these pages will help reshape minds and hearts so that humanity can be changed for the better.

Kalu Onwuka

From a spiritual perch man looks ahead

To the new place of renewal and hope

For backwards leads to a misguided past

To the accusatory and the recriminatory

Chapter 1

WALKING IN LIGHT

Spiritual discernment, though not fully appreciated as should by many, is a very special divine gift that allows mankind to view life from an exalted perch. He that has received this gift will be circumspective in life for he will be given to know in full in any given situation and not in part as many do unfortunately. Such is one who can perceive and have insight into the important in life. With spiritual discernment mankind can not only see the obvious but the concealed as well. The perceptive spirit can sense the little things which matter that the spiritually blind dismiss as inconsequential. He that has this gift will always be at ease in life for he will be immune to those things that trip up the spiritually blind. He can venture forth in life and not lose his way for he is tied by an inseparable cord of love to the Divine as one who lives by faith not sight.

Spiritual discernment bestows the faithful believer with the eye of the spirit so that he can perceive darkness however well concealed. When the enemy of light or the prince of the darkness of this world is revealed through God's proving light he can no longer hurt mankind for he thrives in darkness. When that becomes the case, the enemy loses the ability to choke the flow of the power that enables new life through Christ. The gift of spiritual discernment is much needed for victorious living in these days when the actions of men differ vastly what they say. But such a gift does not come in a spiritual vacuum. He that desires it must first learn to feed and live by Truth through the teachings of Christ Jesus. He who feeds with due diligence will grow in faith and mature in spirit to become the circumspective in spirit. He will gain the key of knowledge and true understanding which makes all things to reveal themselves in light.

He that has received the gift of spiritual discernment must live according to a higher law and for a greater purpose. He must live in God's truth and light so that his spirit can remain free to soar uninhibited to the utmost. He must always look forward and not look backwards. Looking backwards leads to the accusatory and recriminatory past. Looking forward leads to the new place of hope and renewal. He that has the gift of discernment will often be misunderstood and vilified by the spiritually blind. He that has this gift must not bother to defend himself for the future will certainly vindicate and validate him. He is one given to speak and act for the benefit of humanity from the place of informed knowledge. He must never fail to fulfill this mission even though he may be rejected by many. However some will come to embrace Truth and find new life thereby. New life is justification for wisdom and fulfillment realized by the willing. Be that as it may, the perceptive has to learn to forgive and pray for those who reject Truth on account of ignorance and willful blindness. Forgiveness is a divine gift and the means by which the heart becomes circumcised to be lit with the flame of love.

There is no fear in love and therefore in God for he is love. The faithful believer who loves God has nothing to fear when he thinks, speaks and acts out of love for the benefit of humanity and not for personal gain. Many may come against God's beloved one but their opposition will amount to little or nothing at all. Victory in Christ is not given to those who act in their own will and run in blind fury. It is given in mercy by God to the faithful that serve his divine will in love. He that truly loves God will be beloved by Him so that that he will be able to chase away a thousand faithless that plot against him. God's beloved may encounter myriad obstacles but they are enabled to overcome all through faith.

The power of God is without limits and available for those who have found welcome retreat in him through Christ. The Heavenly Father is an omnipresent God who sees and knows all things. His eye rests on the beloved who must strive to give a good account at the end of the day. God gives more from his largesse to him who makes productive use of what he has been given but withholds his hand of blessing from him who does little with it. There is no short-cut or quick-way to be taken when the believer desires to walk in the sunshine of divine love and find new life through Christ Jesus. He who desires the new life and all its peaceable gifts must come in through the lowly gate of the sheepfold. He must come in contrition and humble subservience for that is the way of Christ and the door that connects the seeker to the Heavenly Father.

The faithful believer that walks in the footsteps of Christ will find strength in moments of weakness and help in times of trouble. He will grow in knowledge and wisdom as he settles within the divine sheepfold through truth, light, and love availed through Christ. The Divine Father rewards faithfulness and never fails to provide the faithful with whatever he lacks and needs. Therefore the follower after Christ must strive to be devoted and remain faithful so that he will be in good stead with the Heavenly Father always. He must first seek after the kingdom of God and be certain of his place within the divine fold before seeking earthly things. He must set his spiritual house in order so that he may receive the good and perfect gifts to fill each room of his life as necessary.

God never fails to keep his promises and will always meet the needs of the faithful. The believer that is faithful in his walk will surely pass through the door of Christ to come into the Heavenly Father. When that happens, he becomes one for whom the Divine has prepared a table and will always find green pasture to nourish him in mind, body and spirit. He that feeds from the table that God has prepared will never lack in the good and perfect gifts. He will begin a new life on the parkway of mercy where the fulfilling and enduring are divinely availed. He has become part of God's plans for the new heaven on earth and a light to show others the way as a vanguard of the age of Christ. The age of Christ is the fulfillment of the ascendance of the spirit and demise of the flesh. It is the awaited golden age of humanity reserved for only those who have been remade in the divine image to be spiritually fit. Therein God has saved the best for last for those reborn in light through Christ and filled with the divine anointing.

The unbeliever who rejects Christ and seeks fulfillment through any other means will be disappointed. The best that he can obtain will be material goods. The latter will not satisfy for mankind's hunger is within and can only be met spiritually. Such a faithless one can acquire possessions but that will turn out to be fool's gold in the end when it truly counts. He will neither find fulfillment nor consolation in his possessions. The latter will take him into further estrangement from God and away from true fulfillment. He may be seemingly rich in worldly goods but his hunger for more will never cease. In rejecting the door of Christ, he has chosen the contention and emptiness of wantonness over contentment with godliness. For such a faithless one, dissatisfaction and vexation within will be the bane of his life.

There is a spirit within or the inner man resident within every person. However the spirit or the inner man remains dormant or 'spiritually dead' unless awakened to new life. The only means to bring the spirit within man back to life is by the grace of God through faith in Christ Jesus. The believer that embraces the way of Christ will be afforded redeeming grace. For many the spirit within will never be awakened to life due to unbelief and lack of faith. These faithless ones choose to reject the message of Christ and decline God's offer of redemption for mankind by grace through faith. Nevertheless many have believed and embraced the message of Christ to find God's promises to be so true. These faithful ones have been awakened to new life in spirit through Christ. Not all who are so awakened in spirit will grow to full maturity in Christ. However a select number earmarked by the Heavenly Father among professed believers will have the awakened spirit within grow from infancy to full spiritual maturity in Christ. These are the elect ones chosen to undergo full spiritual transformation in the way. They will grow and mature on the path of righteousness into knowledge of the Heavenly Father. Such will get to experience the full power availed through the blood of the Lamb of God both to redeem mankind as well as afford salvation as due.

For those in whom the spirit within remains dead the lust of the flesh will dictate all their actions. For those who have believed and found strong faith, it is no longer the lust of the flesh but the spirit awakened within that governs them. For them, the flesh has become subservient to the spirit or the inner man within. The inner man is nourished by Truth embodied in the teachings of Christ Jesus. His teachings embody the word of God or Truth in its most expedient form available to the seeker. It is the most potent food that man can receive to transform his spirit and change his nature for the better. Christ Jesus is the encapsulation of the Divine mind availed to mankind. He that faithfully takes the vitamin capsule of the Christ message will become firm in spirit. Such might even become a son in due season if it is divinely appointed for him. For this reason Christ Jesus is 'Emmanuel' which is to say the embodiment of God among those that receive him in good faith. The believer that embraces and lives by the teachings of Christ will grow in faith and mature in spirit to become an 'Emmanuel' as well if it has been so ordained for him by the Heavenly Father. The faithful that has been transformed into an 'Emmanuel' is a son of God given to walk under the mantle of Divinity on earth.

The teachings of Christ Jesus embody the spirit of new life on to the Divine. Such springs into life to grow into full maturity in the heart where it has been received in good faith. It is akin to transferring the embryo of 'Emmanuel' into the believer. The embryo will develop and mature into adulthood within the believer in due season with faithful diligent care. The inner man matured to adulthood within the believer is the same 'Emmanuel' as the parent from which it was taken. It is in effect spiritual cloning in the likeness of the Divine. It is bestowing mankind with the essence of godliness. The faithful who has 'Emmanuel' dwelling within shines forth as light. It is the light of God that shines within him and will draw many to the Heavenly way. Such a host to 'Emmanuel' must be willing and ready to give of himself to all who are drawn to him. He must open the door of his heart to anyone that knocks. Those who will come to knock thirst for the living water of life that flows out of 'Emmanuel' but sourced from the Father of all above. Such a fountain of new life must remain full and free to the seeker so that no one is denied.

The embryo of 'Emmanuel' dwells for a season under the dark clouds of the obscured self and seemingly under the silence of Heaven. In that season, he is in the cocoon of love which is the womb of spiritual transformation in the divine way. After the season is completed, the dark clouds burst into glorious sunshine with the Divine always at hand to bless. Such a host has become prepared and readied for service to all as 'Emmanuel' reborn. He in whom the 'Emmanuel' within has grown to full maturity in this wise is an intercessor given to hold the power for forgiveness and judgment as a divine proxy on earth. God will duly honor his requests but he must do all that God asks of him.

Chapter Notes

- ✓ The faithful views life from a spiritual perch and balances the spiritual with the earthly well.
- ✓ To look backwards leads to recrimination but to look forward leads into hope and renewal.
- ✓ The faithful believer who thinks, speaks and acts in love for the benefit of all has nothing to fear in life.
- ✓ The faithful must set his spiritual house in order so that he may receive good gifts to fill each room.
- ✓ The faithful will begin to live gloriously in new life when the spirit becomes ascendant over the flesh.
- ✓ The faithless that rejects Truth choses contention and emptiness over contentment with Godliness.
- ✓ The teaching of Christ is the encapsulation of the mind and love of God for mankind to receive.
- ✓ The words of Truth spring to life and to full maturity if welcomed into the heart in good faith.
- ✓ The man whose spiritual eye God has opened is given bravery of heart and inner strength.
- ✓ The dark clouds burst in tender mercies when God is near to bless.
- ✓ The fountain of Christ must remain full and free to the seeker so that no one is denied.

The new man reborn in greater love

Gets to live in immunity of godliness

For the past has been made impotent

And powerless to harm Destiny's own

Chapter 2

IN THE FOOTSTEPS AND HEARTBEAT

The more the believer lives in accordance to Truth is the more that he gets filled with the knowledge and wisdom of God. It is by being faithful and obedient to Truth that mankind can start on the path of spiritual ascension. Spiritual ascension is the figurative mounting up with the wings of the eagle to the exalted realm where the saintly commune with the Divine. The latter is the place where the earthly can rise to meet the heavenly in an embrace of love and comfort. The faithful whose spirit within is able to ascend to that exalted meeting point becomes one who is forever changed. His perspective of the world will never be the same for he will begin to see the total picture and no longer in part as most people do. The total picture comprises both the earthly and the heavenly component of life. He that can see the full picture becomes both circumspective and insightful in all his dealings with his fellow man. He has been given to take the high road for he becomes aware of mankind's shortsightedness and the spiritual blindness of many. Such has become a traveler on the road less travelled that many seek but only a few find. The road less-travelled in this light is the path appointed for the righteous before God where the divine hand is ever near to guide mankind's footsteps.

He that has mounted up with the wings of the eagle will be bestowed with divine wisdom. He that has the vision of the eagle is able to eat the meat of Truth and given to see the picture concealed within things. He can sort out that which matters in life and know to leave the unimportant alone. The lofty spiritual heights to which he soars is the domain of the life bearing rain clouds. Most men, including many who profess to follow after Christ Jesus, trudge along close to the valley spiritually. They traverse the well beaten and familiar tracks. They are not able to mount up to the rain bearing clouds. They intersperse themselves among the low cloud vapors which bear no rain. The low clouds are quickly dispersed hither and thither by the prevailing winds of the times. The low cloud is the milk of the word that is subject to myriad interpretations and by which many seekers of Christ are misled. This area is where many 'churches and denominations' of the world gouge on the spiritually ignorant. All who dwell in the valley will not grow to mature spiritually but will be spiritual dwarfs unable to enter into the kingdom of God.

The life bearing clouds are found high up in the mountains. There are densely pervaded in purity with the dew of life and mists of wisdom. It is a holy place that only the exalted in spirit are allowed into. The mountain is the holy mount of God where only the pure in heart can ascend. He that is able to mount up there is baptized and soaked in the dew of life. The spirit of life will pervade all his being and never leave him. He will become the immortal in spirit who the dew of life follows from the mountain down to the valley as called to do God's work. He can soar up interminably between the mount to soak up the dew and come down again to the valley to bring new life to the parched and thirsty willing to receive. Such has become a rain-man engaged in the eternal dance of the cycle of life performed in sync with the divine heartbeat.

God is always doing a new thing in his never ending process of perfecting man. It is like purifying gold. An assay of one hundred percent purity is hoped for but unattainable because the flesh precludes that. A threshold of ninety percent is acceptable for God's divine purposes. The teaching and words of the Christ Jesus purifies and brings man to the threshold of ninety percent. Beyond that threshold is the new place where the Heavenly Father communes with his sons. It is in the region between ninety and hundred percent that God the Father intermeddles with mankind. It is the place where God seeks out man's company in the cool of the day. The cool of the day is when the sun cannot smite God's chosen ones. It is when the faithful become justified before God and are imputed with Divine righteousness. It is the time appointed for the exalted in spirit to do the glorious on earth as ordained in Heaven. It is in the place of communion between God and the sons that Eden can be found and farmed. It is in the garden where the patriarch and his sons commune that Divine power is showcased. It is the place of the fruitful, fulfilling and enduring fruits where nothing can hide for all things glow in lovely purity.

He that seeks ascension to the exalted heights desires a place on Heaven's tableland and so must be willing to sacrifice everything for love of God. Much like Aaron he must desire to be on God's side always so that his beard and loins will remain covered with the white dew of the divine anointing. He must be willing to make a total commitment to serve with his life and become fitted to offer up sacrifices as well as receive gifts from God on behalf of humanity. He is called to be an elect one that God listens to. He has no past life for his yesterdays are no more. He has become a new man in God by light of Truth imparted through Christ who now has an endless future.

The future beckons the reborn in light through Christ with much hope and promise. He must leave the corruptible and worldly for such are leashes that keep earthbound. To remain free to soar in spirit, mankind must forget the things of the past for there are dead weights that encumber the soul and drag many down. To look back to the mistake-filled past keeps man a victim. But to look to the future makes him to be victorious in life. To be free to soar to the heavenly heights is God's gift to the faithful for therein is ordained the conversation that uplifts humanity. Up there is where mankind becomes privy to the veiled and sacred truths which he must use for the works of divine glory as well as help guide others on to the heavenly path.

He that commits his life to serve God and goodness enters into a covenant with the Heavenly Father. This is the covenant of the son who has left his own worldly pursuits to come home and run the Father's business. This is the covenant of Christ. The Father's business is to show the children of the valley who dwell in the shadows how to soar in spirit to the summit through faith in Christ. The faithful son of covenant is chosen to be the elect through whom the grace of God will flow to those who seek after righteousness. He is the elect of God who has laid down his life to bear the people's infirmities and to carry the scourge of their sins on account of love as well as life. The son of covenant can enter into the veiled place through grace and obtain from God in mercy to share with the needy. He may well be received with doubt, derision and despised by many but time inevitably vindicates him.

The trash of humiliation and rejection piled upon the elect ones affords divine protection. The Father uses the base and despised things of the world to confound those who are wise in their own eyes. The trash of rejection piled on every elect one protects him just as Egypt protected the innocent child of glory from the fury of Herod. The obsolete misguided past remains impotent to harm God's elect ones for they are immunized in godliness and bestowed with goodness as sustenance for the future.

The faithful that is able to ascend from the valley to the summit of God's mountain has joined the divine family. He has embarked on the journey of the deified in spirit who walks among men but dwells in spirit with the Heavenly Father. Though his spirit soars to the great heights yet he performs his worthy service on earth so that the thirsty garden of humanity's soul may be refreshed in new life. It is a two-step dance. First he offers up sacrifices well-received above through selfless acts on behalf of humanity. Such are the sacrifices well received above for there are not performed for the praise of men but out of a pure heart on account love for God and goodness.

Next the Heavenly Father grants his petitions for he prays in faithfulness with due thanksgiving for what is best and needed for the day. This is the rain dance of life by which the good and perfect gifts are received. The faithful who lives to serve God and humanity in this wise is the true custodian who is diligently rehabilitating Eden from humanity's sunset to its new sunrise. He is one given to reverse the curse of man's yesterdays and replace it with the hopeful promise of tomorrow. He is one who the hand of wisdom guides to erase the mistake of Adam and to replace it with the 'retake' of Christ.

All who can ascend up the mountain of faith live on earth as men but dwell above in spirit within the congregation of the justified before God through Christ. By them and in them, Christ is very well alive and carrying on the Heavenly Father's work on earth. By them the walls of darkness are being torn down so that divine light can shine into men's hearts all over the world. Only such can declare boldly that Christ has come alive for they know that he has come to full life within them.

When Christ has come to full maturity within the devoted believer, he emerges from within when the occasion arises to lead him forward in his earthly walk. He emerges so that the misguided past of the yesterdays can be severed and the full promise of tomorrow can be realized. The yesterdays of life attempt to hold back from the promise of the future. The yesterdays of life are the hurts and wounds of broken promises. There are the disappointments of unfulfilled dreams. The wounds of yesterday though buried deep within can be soothed and healed by the balm of the divine anointing through Christ. Only Christ can soothe the wounds of life so that they no longer define the faithful believer. Christ emerges from within to urge the faithful to fear not but come along to rendezvous with the Divine and destiny's fulfillment. Christ emerges to lead into Providence where man's true destiny is manifested and realized. Christ within emerges to lead so that the faithful can finally stand firm to be counted among the righteous.

It is by faithfulness that the believer learns to banish his fears. He in whom Christ has come to full life no longer has anything to fear but must set his mind on the things above. There is no fear up above where the spirit is free to excel. Where there is no fear, love is perfected and abounds. It is only in the exalted heights as man becomes truly focused on the Heavenly that he can realize the perfection of godliness ordained for him. There are no yesterdays to be found in the starry heights but the limitless expanse of tomorrow. The clusters of grace are found on the lower branches of the tree of life but the choice grapes of mercy are obtained on the uppermost boughs. The faithful believer is nourished through the fears of his infant days with the cluster of grace in the lower branches. But when Christ comes to full maturity, he can reach up to the uppermost boughs to find the choice and tender grapes of mercy that abound there.

Chapter Notes

- ✓ The believer that lives in faithfulness to Truth will be duly filled with knowledge and divine wisdom.
- ✓ The lofty realm to which the faithful soar in spirit is the domain of new life.
- ✓ The believer able to ascend up the Holy mount of God will be baptized and soaked in the dew of life.
- ✓ God is long suffering and does new things for the perfection of the faithful in an unending process.
- ✓ The faithful reborn in full light has no past for his yesterdays are no more but his future is endless.
- ✓ The past things are dead weights that drag down the spirit and preclude the promises of the future.
- ✓ The scorn, humiliation and rejection of the faithful afford divine immunity in the long-term.
- ✓ The faithful that serves humanity in the light of true love is a kindler of the embers of Hope.
- ✓ God uses the elect to tear down walls of darkness so that divine light can shine through for all.

The flame of love highlights the way

In ascents and descents up the ladder

As lights that twinkle in labors of love

To and fro between heaven and earth

Chapter 3

A UNIVERSAL LANGUAGE

Wisdom declares that there should be no fear in love as perfect love casts away all fears. It is such perfect love that permeates the starry and heavenly heights where the spirits of just men congregate. Many have become justified before God by willingly sacrificing much in love so that others may come into the knowledge of the Divine as should. The believer justified before God in this wise is the good shepherd who lives for goodness and godliness. Such is a proven and worthy partaker of grace through Christ who has grown to be free in spirit and rid of fears. But he that partakes unworthily of grace in that he seeks after own gain, recognition or the praise of men will never be rid of fear and doubt. He will continue to have doubts and fears because he has not been immunized in the purity of Truth. His spirit will never be free for he lives a shadowy life and not in true light. Such will always be uncertain in his ways for fear and doubt will bedevil to ground him in his undertakings.

Mankind can only know the true self in the reflection of Truth. He that desires to know his true self must embrace Truth. The teachings of Christ Jesus embody Truth that sets the spirit free. It peels away the outer garment of the flesh so that the inner man can have the needed room to fill out and blossom to full life. Truth puts the flesh on a leash to set it at naught but releases the inner man so that it may begin the transformative journey of spiritual ascendancy. It is by this process that the flesh yields in submission to the inner man of the spirit within. It is by this process that the flesh is diminished so that the spirit can fully abound. It is the inner man of the faithful believer that matures to be in communion with the Heavenly Father and shines forth to be duly perceived.

The faithful believer in whom the spirit of the inner man has grown to full maturity becomes adopted as a son by God. The spirit within such is in similitude and of same kindred as Christ Jesus the first born son of God. He is an offshoot of the same branch with the potential to do in kind as Jesus did during his time on earth. Every one adopted as a son is given to live in the kingdom of God. The kingdom of God is realized by the faithful believer matured in Christ as he is guided in his endeavors to do on earth as done in Heaven. All who are so guided are in effect re-creating a new earth in which things are patterned after the order of those in heaven.

All who dwell within the realm of God's kingdom are given

to be of one mind. It is a mind always in agreement with the Heavenly Father. The Divine spirit governs the believer in truth, light, love and life to avail a mindset that resists the devilish as well as expose spiritual ugliness wherever such lurks. He who has matured in spirit to be in agreement with the Divine always is an ark of the covenant of God chosen to spearhead earthly battles through faith in Christ. Wherever the ark of covenant leads is where the Divine is put first in life's endeavors. It is this divine impulse that enables the sons all over the world to remake their environs to God's liking. The size, shape and color may vary but it is the same within each son for it is an ark whose content never changes. It is the never changing impulse of light to overcome darkness. It is the Holy Ghost informing and the Holy Spirit leading the faithful to carry out God's will to Heaven's good pleasure.

The faithful who lives in the kingdom of God is given to have a foretaste of the new Heaven on earth. His way of life may be viewed as being outside of today's norm but it will be the way of the new earth to come for the unseen hand of God guides his way. It is a life that demands a very short leash on the flesh so that the spirit can flourish to the utmost. The spirit must be in full flourish and tuned in spirit to hear for the Heavenly Father is revealing so much in these times wherever Christ reigns as sovereign.

As there is proliferation of general knowledge both good and evil in today's world so also is a great unveiling of the veiled Truth to seekers taking place in the spiritual realm. This is the season for man to come into true knowledge. The stars of heaven have lit up to cover all corners of the night sky. The divine edict has been written over the night sky and the counter is about to reset. The stars of heaven are the exalted souls that can understand the hidden truths and divine mysteries. They have been given spiritual sight so that they can understand the divine mind for the benefit of their short sighted fellows. They are the sons of light prepared and situated by God all over the world. They foretell of things to come so that those that dare to embrace Truth may come into the safety of God's ark with them.

He that has been fully transformed in spirit through Christ is a torch lighted with the flame of divine love. Light does not need to make any noise in order to attract attention. He that desires to see must gravitate towards light. The closer that one gets to it is the clearer that one sees. The flame of love speaks inaudibly in twinkles of light divinely induced by the ascent and descent of messengers to and fro between heaven and earth. Knowledge that is borne below is worldly and a tinkling cymbal that makes much noise to lead mankind further into darkness and away from the Divine. In today's world where the actions of many differ from what they say, the wisdom from above affords mankind the means to discern the true intentions of men. It is indeed divine light that can make the erstwhile blind to see and choose wisely in all things.

As mentioned earlier, the faithful that becomes fully matured in Christ becomes duly adopted as a son of God. Such is one who will be soaked in the mists of time and wisdom. He will have knowledge of things to come and also have the distilled knowledge of past ages afforded him. In effect he can travel back through time and yet can travel into the future. In this light, he has become timeless for he is one that travels back and forth through time. He is able to travel backwards because he is linked in spirit with the saints that have gone before. He is able to travel into the future because he is linked with the mind of God through Christ Jesus. The latter is the first born son of this order who showed those willingly to embrace Truth the way to realize eternity or timelessness. Many have embraced to mature in the way of light to join him and as well as others in this order of the divine household appointed for the faithful among all peoples of the earth.

The order of the divine household of the most holy God is timeless and cuts a parabolic arc over humanity. All the wisdom of man's ancient past has been distilled and encapsulated in the teachings of Christ Jesus. It can purify the most depraved soul to make the foulest man clean to stand before God in due time. It can also tame the wild beast in man so that he can become housebroken to live in peace with all. The way of Christ is the filtering medium by which debased man is purified into a reborn spiritual being. Christ Jesus affords mortal man the way to join the rank of divinity for whosoever masters the way becomes a 'Christ-Man' or one christened to walk under divine light. Such is one given to walk under Heaven's cloak among humanity for he has become an arm of the divine impulse on earth.

God affords his sons tender mercies and requires same of them towards blind men. It costs the faithful believer almost everything to grow into full spiritual maturity in Christ. He that has matured in Christ must never be focused on fame or fortune in order to serve worthily. He must be willing to bear the marks of the hatred of the world for love of Truth and goodness. He must be willing to live without due reverence from those for whom he labors to share true light. He must be willing to be taken advantage of by men and yet be falsely accused by the same. He will be robbed and left for dead by the capricious. Yet he is called to forgive the ignorance of the spiritually blind. He must be willing to bless where he has been cursed, to give where he has been robbed and to help where he has been denied. It all seems like a tall order and sounds impossible but with God all things become possible. It is the mountain of faith that has to be scaled to the summit and it is only possible with the divine wind to lend aid to the seeker. He who seeks must be merciful so that the stream of divine mercy can remain open for him. There is no way to get around this fact within the divine economy. The divine gifts flow outwards in ripples generated from the core of mercy that defines God's heart but finds only the merciful and pure of heart.

Without a doubt, the fully matured in Christ suffers much injustice in the world. It is the price that the world demands of him who must abandon her to become a son of God. It is the figurative thirty pieces of silver that the world considers to be a fair price for he that seeks to be righteous before God. The faithful must be willing to make that payment so that he can be awakened in the spiritual image of the Heavenly Father. He that is awakened in the image of the Divine will become connected to the realm of wisdom and true knowledge. He will become connected to the possessor of all things both in Heaven as well as on earth to enter into a season of the good and perfect in his life. He who has willingly paid the price of ransom can afford to speak to the injustice in the world for nothing can harm his spirit anymore. He must speak to bring down the institutions of darkness in high places. He must speak to expose and make the walls of spiritual ugliness to tumble down for much power lies in his words.

To be worthy of his calling, the fully matured in the way must dedicate his life to help bring others into the knowledge of the Divine. He that has knowledge of the Divine lives in fulfilled hope. He has passed from the darkness of the earthly side into the light of the heavenly side to experience the reality of God in very intimate ways. Such who has grown from faith to fulfilled hope must continue in same light and grow from hope to charity. Charity endures and never gives up even as God the Father endures. Charity is the essence of godliness and of the

A Universal Language

kindred of divinity. Charity and mercy are divine twins that are often difficult to tell apart. Charity is that which enables the divine dynamic in the faithful believer to speak to the core of all things and produce desired outcomes. Mercy affords a pure heart so that the roots of bitterness will not take hold within. A pure heart will always produce good fruits for such is a divine garden.

Charity is a divine vehicle that will pick up and bring the believer closer to the heart of God. Charity speaks the universal language of love. It is the great utility vehicle able to do all things and go anywhere in the universe. It is the currency of the truly noble in spirit. Charity is the creature perfected in the cocoon of love that is the bowel of Christ. It embodies all things that are good in the eyes of God. It is the measure of the golden rule that will govern the new Heaven on earth. Charity must never be contrived, feigned or abused. At its best, it is a burnt sacrifice offered up effacingly that pleases the Heavenly father very much. The light of charity shines out brightly from the heart where it abounds. Charity does not parade itself, seek for praise, clamor for attention or seek recognition. It does not need a stand for it cannot be hidden or obscured. True charity does not need to pose to be noticed for the universe seeks it out and bows to it.

Chapter Notes

- ✓ Perfect love permeates the lofty realm where the spirits of those justified before God congregate.
- ✓ The word of Truth sets the flesh at naught and puts it on a leash so that the spirit can abound.
- ✓ Life in the kingdom of God is for the faithful who have come to full spiritual maturity through Christ.
- ✓ Earthly endeavors are blessed when the Holy Ghost informs and the Holy Spirit enables the believer.
- ✓ The faithful that has become a son of God is soaked in the mists of wisdom and framed by love.
- ✓ Wisdom past, present and future are encapsulated in the teachings of Christ.
- ✓ Divine gifts and blessings flow outwards in ripples that are generated from the core of God's heart.
- ✓ The suffering that the faithful endures is the price that the world demands of him who abandons her.
- ✓ True charity embodies the spirit that does not seek notice yet the universe seeks it out and bows to it.
- ✓ Charity is a divine vehicle that dutifully lifts up and brings the faithful closer to the heart of God.
- ✓ The universe seeks out and bows to the heart wherein Charity makes a home.
- ✓ Charity is a measure of the golden rule that will govern the new heaven on earth.

The divine way is much purer and better

Disconnected from man's earthly ways

Realm where the shadowy becomes real

And darkness holds no stakes or claims

Chapter 4

THE ULTIMATE VICTORY

The believer who truly desires to realize the divine gifts availed through Christ must be faithful in obeying God's laws. The laws embody the commandments as well as the covenant, statutes and ordinances. It should be noted first and foremost that no man can meet all those requirements without spiritual help. Mankind can have the spiritual help needed through belief and obedience to the teachings of Christ Jesus. The requirements for meeting the laws of God will be met as the seeker faithfully follows in the way after Christ in sincerity and humility. The believer that follows faithfully will grow to mature in spirit and meet up with Christ in due season in accordance with God's will. He that has met up with Christ in this light has become justified in God's eye and fulfilled the requirements of all the laws.

To meet up with Christ is to be spiritually borne into divine light. Without the fulfillment of the laws, one cannot meet up with Christ for that is the realm of divinity and all that are righteous before God. To put it briefly, one cannot become unless he has and yet cannot have unless he is. It all sounds much like a bridge too far for mankind to cross. Yet it is the bridge of destiny that each person must cross in order for mankind to connect with the Divine. But through the magnanimity of God's love, the believer that has not can have through grace and the faithful that is not can become under mercy.

The answer to the puzzle is to be found through Christ Jesus. The laws of God are not technical but spiritual. Christ is the realization of mankind's spirit perfected in godliness. The believer who masters and lives in accordance with the teachings of Christ Jesus will be duly imputed with righteousness in accordance with God's will. Such has become a 'Colossus' of faith whose inner man has duly grown to full spiritual maturity in Christ through grace. The believer that seeks to be like Christ Jesus must embrace his teachings and yield to be led in spirit to pattern his life after him. He that seeks not after his own gain but seeks after the goodness of humanity above all else will be duly availed the Holy Spirit to guide his steps accordingly. It is in this way that mankind is led to become a 'Colossian' in faith and a branch of righteousness.

For the follower of Christ to mature in spirit and become a Colossus of faith, he has to persist through trials, tribulations, humiliation and rejection by the world. He will come to know and accept the fact that he has to suffer for faith. He will know and accept the fact that the world will oppose him in every way it can for the way of Christ runs contrary. Notwithstanding, he will come to meet up with his spiritual quest in due season if he endures. He will meet up with Christ to become a Colossus to be christened in the divine way. Unbeknown to him, through belief and obedience to his teachings, he has reached out and grabbed on to the outstretched hands of Christ. In so doing he will find himself pulled over the divide and across the bridge far beyond man's reach to traverse on his own. By this mystery of grace which flows from God through his sons, the seeker that has been pulled over destiny's bridge or 'saved' becomes a son divinely empowered to pull others across as well. Every son of God has met the requirements of the law and can be a savior to others.

No man can cross the bridge of destiny that separates the temporal and the eternal by his efforts alone. It is the great gulf that separates man from the Divine. It takes a giant spiritual leap that is beyond the capability of man's flesh to accomplish. Man has to have help from a higher spiritually source in order to accomplish this feat. He has to be pulled over by one who is securely anchored on the heavenly side but yet can reach across to the earthly side of the divide to help all earnest seekers. It takes one who is 'saved' to help save others. The sons of God are his proxies that live and walk among men on earth under the cloak of divinity. All such are anchored on the heavenly side of the spiritual divide but live to serve God on earth.

The believer that has been helped across from the earthly to the heavenly side has met the righteousness of God and can also help others who sincerely seek to come across as well. But it is all worked out through divine sovereign will as manifested in both the helper and receiver of help.

The commandments, covenant, statutes and ordinances are for the earthly side of the spiritual divide. The faithful believer that has been helped across to the other side has met the requirements for them. God then requires such to live under very different and higher laws. He is required to live in humility, sincerity and at peace with all men. He is called to share the wisdom which many lack and need on the earthly side. He must not allow the roots of bitterness to take hold in his heart for he now lives in the bowel of God's mercy. He must model the way of Christ as spiritually guided in the hope that other men can learn from him. He is called to speak and do in the same spirit as Christ Jesus his model would with thanksgiving to God always. The believer that is faithful in this wise soon becomes a living showcase for the efficacy of grace, the timeliness of mercy and the amazing power of God.

The commandments, covenants, statutes and ordinances are rudimentary requisites that are useful in honing the faith of the believer. Each of the above comes to bear at certain places and seasons during the spiritual maturation of the believer. Such are regimens that are of tremendous assistance to the believer in that they teach endurance in the way and strengthen the muscles of faith. The journey of spiritual maturation is transformational and life's ultimate marathon. Without the endurance borne of strong faith and belief in God's laws, no believer can get close enough to reach out and grab the hand of Christ as appointed for him. It is to God's glory and utmost wisdom that the laws prove to be of inestimable value in helping the believer grow in faith as he progresses through spiritual transformation.

A commandment is a directive that must be obeyed regardless of prevailing circumstances or how discouraging things may look. Some commandments demand that the believer take certain actions. Other commandments ask the believer to abstain from certain actions. The commandments of God are not limited to the ten listed in the Holy Bible but exceed those to comprehensively include all things that one might consider to be displeasing to God. The purity of the heart and the state of the spirit within goes a long way to determine what one considers to be displeasing or not. God knows that and makes accommodation for spiritual blindness borne of ignorance but he will not countenance willful disobedience.

The ten commandments of Moses are rudimentary in nature. The bars are set very low so that every person who aims for goodness and loves Truth can be able to fulfill them. But yet many in the world struggle to fulfill the laws of Moses. The truth is that most people are not able to fulfill the spirit within those simple laws. It is only when the spirit within has been awakened to full life that mankind is able to fulfill the laws through strong faith. As already noted, the laws are not technical but spiritual in nature. It is quite fruitless and like chasing after his own shadow for man to engage in a spiritual battle with the tools of the flesh. Victory in life is won or lost in the spirit. The strong of faith are well-fitted for the inevitable battles of life but the infirm in spirit are ill-prepared for same.

Oftentimes God asks the faithful believer to do or not do certain things. Any directive of God to the faithful that requires some form of action or abstinence is a commandment. Every believer who remains faithful in his walk will receive commandments from God as he begins to mature in faith. In that case, the commandments will be clearly defined and without ambiguity. The faithful will know with certainty in his heart to do certain things and not to do others. Commandments are directives that help teach the believer the orderliness of the divine mind. The Heavenly Father is an orderly God and heaven an orderly place.

The journey of spiritual transformation is an exercise in taking one guided step after another to bring the believer closer to the heart of God. It is the walk of faith that leads the believer through tribulations to teach him patience, afford him spiritual experiences and thereby bring him to realize hope. Hope is the state where the believer's faith rests in knowledge of the reality of God. Hope is realized when the believer comes to know that God exists with the certainty and assurance that nothing can change. Only when Hope is realized can the believer dutifully and faithfully obey as God commands. Obedience to God's commands constitutes righteousness. Failure to obey constitutes a sin in the eyes of God. The things done or left undone by the believer before he receives a commandment do not constitute sin. It only becomes a sin after he has received the commandment that clearly defines for him what to do or not do. In the divine way, two people can commit the same act and only one is deemed to be a sinner if he has prior knowledge that the act is unlawful.

The issue of sin is often times misunderstood. However the faithful who truly loves and has given his heart to God will go to great lengths to please him. He will give more than is needed. He will go beyond the call of duty. Such is always the case when true love dictates an action for then no cost is too high. The ten commandments of Moses do not constitute the template for fulfilling the righteousness of God. There are given as an early guide to teach the believer that God operates on certain defined principles. God will duly let the faithful believer know what those principles and rules are in timely order. The faithful must obey them for through obedience will he obtain the knowledge and wisdom that will come to guide his life. He will come to know that within God's words is found the governing spirit that leads mankind into the divine stream of the kingdom of light and love.

Oftentimes a commandment may not make sense to the believer because of mankind's limited understanding. God knows in totality but man knows in part. Obedience to his command is the mark of good citizenship in the kingdom of God. It is the desire of every good son to please God for he knows that the Heavenly Father does indeed know best. As mentioned earlier, the believer who faithfully obeys as God commands becomes the righteous before him. Righteousness is not defined by the so-called good deeds of man but by the actions that man takes in obedience to the commanding will of God.

All of man's deeds done outside of God's will, even if lauded and showered with accolades by men, are nothing but earthly props. The believer's endeavors and activities have to be directed by divine will so that such can help into building up God's kingdom. All of man's endeavors are pointless and vain glorious exercises unless those efforts are orchestrated by the spirit of God as part of the divine edifice. He that aspires to build for God must first receive both a building permit and plan from the divine mind.

Chapter Notes

- ✓ The seeker that has met up with Christ has fulfilled the requirements and is justified before God.
- ✓ The seeker that has met up with Christ has realized the perfecting of the spirit through light and love.
- ✓ The seeker that desires full spiritual maturity has to persist through trials, humiliation and rejection.
- ✓ The chosen are living showcases for the efficacy of grace, timeliness of mercy and Divine power.
- ✓ God's laws are regimens that build up the muscle of faith, teach endurance and nourish the spirit.
- ✓ Most men are not able to live up to God's laws for lack of a humble and sincere spirit within.
- ✓ Faithfulness is to yield to God's will and follow as led in spirit regardless of how things appear to be.
- ✓ Spiritual transformation is a step-by-step exercise that brings the seeker closer to the heart of God.
- ✓ The believer that loves Truth will go to great lengths and not count costs to please God.
- ✓ Righteousness is not defined by good deeds but by actions taken in obedience to God's will.
- ✓ He that aspires to build for God must first receive a building permit and then a plan from him.

Takes certainty of faith to live in obedience

To what man knows in his heart to be true

For faithfulness is about the good promise

That counts no costs or hurt to be fulfilled

Chapter 5

STANDING FIRM

An act of covenant is a voluntary decision made by the believer to perform an act of sacrifice that involves some discomfort, material deprivation or denial to the flesh as an affirmation of faith. It may be in the form of abstinence from those wants and fleshly desires that come between the believer and God. As a child of covenant, the believer is led to disavow certain things and actions. He makes the choice to live his life a certain way in order that he may be able to focus on God and walk in the assurance of his divine blessing. In essence, it is an affirmation of faith by which the believer makes a commitment to serve God better so that he may receive and nurture a spiritual gift.

An act of covenant makes an unmistakable declaration to all that the believer no longer belongs with the world but with God. It is a supposedly unbreakable contract between man and God that will remain in effect as long as the believer keeps his end of the bargain. The believer that violates the contract does not make the covenant void but it forces God to temporarily withdraw his hand of blessing. The Heavenly Father knows the weakness of man's heart and makes due accommodation for that. He is long suffering and willing to suffer heartbrokenness until the violator repents. When such repentance takes place in sincerity, God's hand of blessing invariably returns to rest on the son of covenant. When man breaks the covenant, it is like turning off a water faucet. When the covenant breaker repents and recommits himself fully to God, the water faucet is turned back on.

The covenant contract is in line with the spiritual injunction to cut off the offending body part if it is the reason for separation between the believer and God. There is always a choke in the life of the believer as an issue that works against faith and offends the Holy Spirit. The net result is a diminishing of the effectiveness of divine power to work mightily in the life of the believer. To overcome this choke or stranglehold on the spirit, it becomes necessary for the believer to make the personal sacrifice to let go of that crippling desire so that faith and divine blessing may abound as should in his life.

The spiritual choke is a cause for uncertainty or infirmity of the spirit within the believer. He that has an infirm spirit cannot stand up to fight and be counted on by God when needed. He may labor mightily in the flesh but he has set his faith to naught. There is always a season during spiritual transformation when the believer must make a choice. This is where the believer must either choose to bow low before God or to fall down to the nemesis of his faith or juggernaut. He that chooses to bow to God is exalted to become a starry soul but he that bows to juggernaut will be brought low to be entrapped in the earthen. This is the 'Achilles' heel of faith highlighted by Samson's weakness for Delilah and the oversized ego of 'King Saul' that leads him to be presumptuous before God.

A statute is a law that God demands of the faithful who has developed into a certain stage in spiritual growth. It has to do with things that the faithful believer should not be doing anymore in order that he might be able to receive the full benefits due him. A statute is for one who has demonstrated his faith in God through many difficulties and against many odds. It is usually for one who loves God sincerely but is not able to progress beyond a certain point due to the interference of the flesh. He may be linked spiritually in an unequal yoke with others in a relationship or activity that is not a sin. But that relationship or activity inhibits his inner man to limit his horizon. When the upward bound is tethered it can never soar into freedom. It cannot rise to the utmost yet it is not truly earthbound resulting in a constant bobbing that is unsettling and destabilizing. The soul thusly tethered is like salt that has lost its savor to be good for nothing really.

A time comes in the spiritual maturation of the believer when God calls him to go beyond where he is. He must be untethered so as to fulfill the call of the Divine for the heavenly obligation trumps the earthly. A statute is for those few who will be ushered into the most holy place of the Divine. It is for those that God desires to lift up much more or 'promote' to a higher order so to say. It is for those that he considers worthy of his company and wants to draw closer to himself. It is for the elect that God has chosen to be the vessels to be filled with the better and be used to do his mighty works on earth. He that is so chosen must maintain a certain spiritual purity and cleanliness so that he may be ready for use at all times.

Heaven points out a statute for the faithful during the last stage of the believer's transformation into the full divine image. A statute is for those who are about to be established through grace on to mercy. It is for the faithful that is about to become God's ambassador to men. It is for the strong of faith chosen to be God's own elect. This is the realm of the Holy Ghost which has to do with veiled knowledge and wisdom privy to only the noblest of souls. The Holy Ghost is the medium for conveying information from Heaven to the chosen faithful. He informs the faithful but does not do work. It takes the Holy Spirit to enable the believer so he can do God's work. The duo of the Holy Ghost and Holy Spirit make possible the mighty works divinely ordained. The believer without the Holy Ghost will not be well informed as to know God's will. He may be an enthusiastic believer but will still remain a blind one likely to end up in a ditch sooner or later.

There are issues that may not be considered as sinful by the believer but he must abstain from them when directed by the spirit of God. Those kinds of issues have to do with the ability to stand firm and be the faithful watchman found worthy by God. The worthy watchman has to be counted on in all seasons and at all times to remain standing for God. In effect, he is a captive but one favored to ride the high places of the earth much like Daniel was in Babylon. He will overcome all his troubles to abound fully in spirit, be able to see, know, and do the amazing wherever life takes him. He will not be judged like the ordinary but like the extraordinary that God has chosen him to be. He that obeys the statute appointed him will be a well-chiseled statue ordained to serve God with dignity, grace and ever-lasting beauty.

An ordinance is given so that God's work on earth may proceed in the right direction and without obstruction. In as much as it is the Holy Ghost that informs the believer, it takes the Holy Spirit to enable him to put the information received into productive use. The work of the Holy Spirit will be hindered where the believer is infirm in his spirit. The believer with an infirm spirit will not be able to walk according to the dictates of the Spirit of God even though he may know the right steps to take. Such is a lame one who has set his eyes on something else other than God. He may be taking a short cut, a quick route or proceeding according to the dictates of his own will. He may be one attempting to do with the flesh that which can only be accomplished in spirit. He will fail to achieve the desired outcome in his endeavors for the hand of God will not be in it. The footsteps of the faithful believer who yields to the Divine are directed in accordance with a certain order. There is a definite pattern and a clear imprint in those endeavors where God's hand is involved. All things divinely purposed have ordained routes and perceivable markers. Sometimes the route may be obvious and easily discernible but at other times it is not. However the faithful seeker will always be led to find and know the right path ordained for him without fail.

God does not want, haste or waste. He meets the believer's needs and helps him endure all things so that such may find fulfillment. The faithful believer has to wait to be informed of God's will so as to be guided in all his ways by the Divine spirit. Christ must always be the pilot so that his life can be configured in the proper order. The life that is configured through Christ spawns the spirit that can soar to the exalted heights where fulfillment awaits mankind in the freedom of the heavenly expanse.

Chapter Notes

- ✓ Voluntary sacrifice or denial is often necessary to subjugate the flesh.
- ✓ An act of covenant declares that the believer no longer belongs with the world but with God.
- ✓ There is a choke in spiritual walk that works against the seeker in that it offends the Spirit of God.
- ✓ The spiritual choke works in the believer as a cause for uncertainty or infirmity of the spirit.
- ✓ There is a season for the believer to go beyond where he is in order to receive the purer and truer.
- ✓ There is a higher spiritual demand placed on the believer that God chooses as his elect one on earth.
- ✓ He that obeys the statute given him will become a living statue filled with dignity, grace and serenity.
- ✓ The infirm spirit is not able to live according to God's law though he knows the right steps to take.
- ✓ Heaven affords man space to write his new name in star dust when he leaves a good mark on earth.
- ✓ The faithful believer lets go of the un-necessary so that he can keep the necessary in life.

God's heart is the mansion grand and lovely

The sons are rooms in many hues and colors

Pieces of his heart remade in love by his will

To be stars that shine under earth's dark veil

Chapter 6

GIVING BACK IN KIND

The love that leads the faithful believer to lay down his life for the benefit of the beloved flock is Charity. It is the sacrifice of inestimable value made so that others can be afforded the chance for spiritual reconciliation and knowledge of the Heavenly Father. It is the hallmark of the sons of God that stand in mercy before him that Charity governs all their actions. They are justified to stand before God not only through obedient faith but by self-less acts of Charity. Such have found new life through Christ and now live so that others may find as well. He that has laid down his life in this wise to be the good shepherd who looks after the sheep will be covered by the investiture of the mantle of Christ. The Heavenly Father will always love him beyond measure and nothing can separate that love. But he that feeds on the flock for his own gain is an evil shepherd who is soon cut off from God's love.

The faithful believer upon whom the investiture of Christ is bestowed is one transformed in spirit from base man to a purified being. He is one 'born again' in that the old self of his inner man has died and a new self in the image of Christ has risen to take its place. It is a dual transformation that changes both the spirit within and also the flesh without. The transformation of the spirit begins first and is followed subsequently by that of the flesh. Both transformations may be likened to the two axis of a cross. The transformation of the spirit may be likened as taking place along the vertical axis and that of the flesh along the horizontal axis. However both transformations are co-functions for as the spirit leads the flesh follows.

The transformation of the spirit within takes place in three stages. The first is the dead or wooden stage. The second is the brazen stage and the third the golden stage. The dead or wooden stage of the spirit is the initial and default state of all mankind due to Adam's transgression in Eden. On account of that, all men are born from the maternal womb into the world as babies tainted by that original sin. No one is exempt or immunized from its effect. All men begin life on earth dead in the spirit of the inner man. Each man lives as dead wood within until he begins a quest for new life in God. The dead wood was once part of a living tree. So also is the dead spirit within man. It was once alive in God in the distant past of Adam until his fall estranged his spirit from that of God. It is Adam's dead spirit or the wooden estranged from God that everyone has within him as he emerges from his mother's womb at birth.

The desire for new life leads on a spiritual quest that takes the seeker from the wooden through the brazen and finally into the golden where reconciliation with God is realized. Reconciliation with God can never take place until the sins of the seeker, beginning from Adam to the present, has been paid for in blood sacrifice that is acceptable to God. This is where Christ Jesus comes in because he is the sacrificial lamb set aside from the foundation of the world as a worthy and sufficient payment for the sins of all men. Adam is the progenitor of spiritual death or estrangement from God. Christ Jesus is the progenitor of the new life or reconciliation with God.

Anyone who confesses and renounces his sin in sincerity, accepts Christ Jesus as the lord of his life and lives in accordance with his teachings can appropriate his blood sacrifice as payment for sin. By taking these steps, such has become a believer in the ability of Christ to jump start his dead spirit back to new life. Where the erstwhile sinner merits Divine approval, his sins will be cancelled for he has been deemed to be sincere in his confession of sin and declaration of faith. In that case, the 'dead' spirit within the believer will be stirred to life and begin the process of rehabilitation or spiritual transformation. Such has gone from the first stage of the wooden and dead where the spirit of Christ is absent to the second stage of the brazen where new life through Christ has been spawned. It is not yet full spiritual transformation but a very good beginning.

The brazen is the middle stage of spiritual transformation. This stage happens to be the end of the journey for most of the professed followers of Christ Jesus. It is the end of spiritual transformation for them but for the chosen earmarked for full spiritual transformation there is more to come. Here in the middle stage, there is an enthused desire to learn the words, psalms and hymns of scripture. However this is the real battle ground of faith. In this stage the believer begins to experience the gifts of the Holy Spirit and to reap the benefits of God's grace through Christ. He is impacted in tangible ways that benefit him not only spiritually but materially as well. He has been spawned as a spiritual baby in the new life of Christ. The baby has to be nurtured, nourished and protected from the things in his environment that will do him harm. It is grace that keeps him safe until he can come to full spiritual maturity and be able to stand on the strength of his own faith before God in mercy.

In essence, grace is the aggregate of services afforded the believer to sustain him while he is still young and growing in faith. Here the word of Truth is broken down as baby food and milk for him by another. This is often done by an elder in the way who is strong of faith and led by the divine spirit to share his spiritual cloak with the younger. The flow of grace continues until the young and growing is able to stand on own feet in faith. But the believer must be a worthy partaker of the grace of God for that maturity of spirit to come about. He must not appropriate grace for selfish gain as many do. The body of Christ is a commonwealth meant to be shared for the common good of humanity. Therefore the partaker should not gouge and over-indulge on the feast of grace. To partake of grace unworthily or selfishly is a slippery slope that leads to an arrested development or spiritual dwarfism. Grace is provisional and meant to cater to the weakness, ignorance and folly of youth. The young is expected to mature in due season and be able to cater not only for himself but hopefully for others who may follow after him as well.

Sadly, many who profess to follow after Christ have become addicted and spiritually stuck in grace. Most followers of Christ are not willing to be weaned away from the indulgence of grace. Therefore they are not able to be established from grace on to mercy. They are not able to become a nipple of grace so that they may succor others in Christ. Grace through Christ has become the narcotics of the Christian way. It is the reason for the spiritual malaise and crisis of faith which many face today. It is the hunger of Titus for the material that has taken him away to 'Dalmatia' in abandonment of the cause. 'Dalmatia' is the state where that which is furnished in purity has been desecrated through greed to become blighted with dark spots. The unworthy partaker of grace dwells in spirit in Dalmatia under the burden of guilt and self-judgment.

The fountain of grace flows as the lifeblood of the body of Christ. Sadly it has been sucked away by the vampires of religion for own gain. God's grace through Christ has been misappropriated and abused by many. These false followers have looted the body of Christ and view grace as windfall to be accumulated as booty for themselves. The Heavenly Father who cannot be pleased with this state of affairs invariably unleashes a spiritual haze to blast 'the booty' of grace accumulated by the selfish with disapproving mildew from time to time. But sadly and regrettably many are not deterred and continue in same course to misappropriate the gift of Christ.

However the true followers after Christ partake of grace worthily. For such, grace affords due knowledge, protection and experience of the Divine through the sacrificial feast availed by Christ. These truly noble souls are the pure in spirit who take only the little that they need but give far more of themselves so that others may also come to know the heavenly way. They are the worthy given to grow to full spiritual maturity and be well received by God under mercy. They are the faithful ones infused with the sweet smelling fragrance of sacrifices well-received above. Such are those chosen for the third and last stage of spiritual maturity as the ones elected to be reborn in divine light as sons of God.

This third and last stage of spiritual transformation is where the believer becomes God's golden vessel. The golden vessels are those who have been adopted as sons. This is the stage of the 'fuller' and 'greater' maturity in

Christ. It is here that the believer becomes a 'Christ-Man' through whom God wills and acts on earth. Such are the ones who gather around God's divine throne in spirit to receive from him in mercy and offer to others in grace. They are attached to the Divine in mercy and are the nipples of grace from which others suck the essence of the new life of Christ. He that has been transformed into this spiritual 'gold' will never change or corrode. A bonding has taken place between him and the Divine that is permanent and irreversible. This bond of love once formed is never broken for the chosen has joined the heavenly throng of spirits that abide forever.

As the faithful believer becomes progressively transformed in the inner man from the wooden to the brazen on to the golden, so does his earthly endeavors progressively change from that of stone to that of iron and finally to that of silver. The wooden or dead spirit devoid of Christ produces works of 'stone'. The brazen spirit that is not yet matured in the way of Christ produces works of 'iron'. But the golden spirit that has the 'fuller' and 'greater' maturity in Christ produces works of 'silver'. It can be clearly seen that with each level of spiritual transformation, the handiwork of man becomes less weighty. Weight has to do with gravity or the degree of attachment that an object or material has to earth. The things that are earthbound are heavier than those that are not.

The work of stone is borne of the wooden or dead spirit

that is devoid of Christ. Stone works however massive and imposing, are cold lifeless tombs that pay homage to the spirit of the precocious dead past. Stone works are 'pyrrhic' victories that take more to accomplish than the reward they afford. The works of stone do not and cannot sing for they are cages for the spirit. Stone works clip man's wings of flight and keep his spirit grounded on earth. Being borne of the wooden spirit that is dead or 'asleep' in the earth, stone works are apt to tumble down to earth for all things must satisfy the primordial urge to return from whence they came forth.

The work of iron is borne of the brazen spirit that has some measure but not full maturity in Christ. It too can indeed be massive and imposing. Although it is less weighty, it will corrode and rust. The work of iron is neither here or there. It is not completely earthbound for it will occasionally rise above the earth to fall back down once more. The work of iron is borne of the brazen spirit that has not yet mastered spiritual flight. The works of iron are overly presumptuous for there are not sustainable, enduring or fulfilling. As a result, the work of iron is often 'ironic' in that it produces an undesirable outcome than was originally intended. The work of iron presumes to 'sing' but it does so with a loud and clattering noise that is disquieting to the spirit.

The nightmare of the industrial age is a fiasco borne of the brazen spirit for it starved man's soul but pampered his flesh. The brazen bites off more than it can chew. The brazen spirit is wasteful and is easily constipated. When the fineries, adornments and bewitching lights of the industrial age are removed, it can be seen that it presumed to set faith in the Divine at naught. When faith is set at naught, material things take over and control man. The erstwhile possessor soon becomes the possessed.

When faith is set at naught, the creature soon proceeds to presume to be his Creator. In effect, it is the less assuming to be greater than the more. When that is the case, it becomes a world turned upside down where darkness presumes to rule over light. The truth of the matter is that the industrial age attempted to close but could not lock the gate to the guild halls of divine wisdom. But sadly and regrettably, it opened the flood gates of human wantonness and moral decadence that has unleashed a dismal flood on mankind that is far beyond his control.

The works of silver are borne of the golden apples of wisdom through those who have been transformed to full spiritual maturity in Christ. The work of silver is not weighty. It is neither massive nor imposing. It easily shakes off the dust of the earth to rise upwards. It will shine before men but will neither corrode nor rust. It is good for all purposes but yet enduring. It is heraldic for it sings subtly but unmistakably of the purity, innocence and hope from which it is borne. The works of silver being borne of the golden in spirit or golden-hearted are well received by the Heavenly Father and duly rise to the home above from whence they originate as twinkling little stars to guide all true seekers through the night passage of the earthly journey.

The works of the golden in spirit or golden-hearted will always be well received and acknowledged by the heavenly Father for the works that they do are directed from above. The golden in spirit have through mastery of the walk of faith come into the fullness of the riches of God through Christ. The golden-hearted no longer walk by sight but are guided in their endeavors to rebuild the broken down, refill the empty and restore the withered. It is by the works of their hands that the Heavenly Father sheds his glory on mankind for he wills and acts through them to bring about much goodness on earth. The golden-hearted have become immunized in godliness and can no longer suffer loss at the hand of the prince of darkness.

Chapter Notes

- ✓ It is the hallmark of all who stand before God in mercy that charity governs all their actions.
- ✓ The spirit is 'dead' in the wooden stage but awake in the intermediate stage of the brazen.
- ✓ Grace sustains the young in faith and abounds in the intermediate stage of spiritual growth.
- ✓ The noble in spirit take only the needed but give far more so that others may share in the Divine.
- ✓ The sons are attached to God in mercy and are nipples of grace from which others are nourished.
- ✓ Handiworks become less earth-centric and weighty but universal and starry with spiritual maturity.
- ✓ Handiworks of the wooden spirit are emblems of the precocious that pay homage to a dead-past.
- ✓ The industrial age is a fiasco borne of the brazen spirit that starves the soul but pampers the flesh.
- ✓ Handiworks borne of the golden spirit evoke the glorious in tones of purity and innocence of hope.

Songs that swell in thankful hearts

In voices tuned to praise in grace

Lift mankind on the wings of joy

Into a realm of sunshine and love

Chapter 7

UNDER SUNSHINE OF LOVE

The believer does not begin his walk with God full of faith. It takes some time to learn to fly on the wings of faith. It takes some time to realize the fullness of riches that faith in God avails through Christ. It takes some time to un-wrap the burial bandages of Lazarus and step out as the fully matured in spirit reborn into full light. He that is fully matured in Christ has become a son of God in heavenly light and will remain so for all ages. Nothing in Heaven above or earth below can separate such from the love of God for he has obtained an irreversible gift. The Heavenly Father will make a cleft so that he can be grafted to the Divine and be able to possess all that his heart desires.

For the faithful believer to be engrafted to the Divine he has to undergo a process of sorting out his life so as to weed out the un-necessary and make room for only the necessary. The pruned life has a lot of re-building to do. But things have to be done in a better light so that there is nothing left to clutter or encumber life. When this is done, he will discover with much joy that his petitions and hearts desires will always be met. The faithful whose heart's desires are readily fulfilled has to set his mind to the lofty standards pleasing to God. It has to be that way so that he can become a 'projector' that makes heavenly things to be realized on earth. He must always have a 'to-do' list that is impressed on his heart. The Spirit of God will search out the items on his 'to-do' list and help to make them come about to his delight. He must make sure that the items on his 'to-do' list will be of a good report before Heaven and earth. If that is the case, then he will find that all that he needs to do will always be carried out to completion. Such a faithful one must make sure to carry out only those 'projects' that serve the cause of godliness and goodness well. If he does that faithfully, he will find that things will be less taxing and expediently done. The days of struggles, shortfalls, short changes and disappointments will be gone.

The season and years of tribulation are divinely ordained to serve the goal of engrafting the believer into the divine stream and will cease once that has been accomplished. They can never be regeneration without tribulation. Before regeneration the faithful believer labors with his mind and flesh. But that will never be enough for all his efforts and endeavors will always fall short of bringing the desired results. The vehicle of that earlier life often disappoints and strands on the way. It can never climb to the top of victory hill or drive out of the miry clay of disappointment valley. But then in regeneration, all things become possible and expedient through the power of the spirit of the Almighty.

The faithful that has come into regeneration has entered into faith-rest with the Heavenly Father. He will find that the vehicle of his life has been retooled into an all-weather utility transport fit for every terrain of life. Such is called to use the retooled vehicle to harness the sunshine of Divine love to do amazing things. He must use the power of that divine sunshine for victorious service on earth to benefit all who are willing to embrace Truth in love. He has become a 'bee' prepared for the propagation of new life through Christ and so has a lot of honeycombs to make to feed those who will be drawn to him. He is one appointed to be the diligent gardener given to tend the seedlings planted in his earthly lot by God. He must get to work and carry on with it for his time has become precious.

Divine love and power to make things happen on earth are harnessed through the power of prayer and earnest entreaty. The 'bee' needs the sunshine of the Heavenly Father's love to produce the pleasing and fulfilling potion of honey. The son that asks not receives not but he that asks will receive in fullness of joy. Such that has come under the sunshine of divine love will enter into rest. The latter is appointed for those received into the company of a host of spiritual helpers to no longer labor on their own. He must therefore set his mind on such things that will exalt him before God. He has become a regenerator and re-creator of the new from the old whose wishes are his divine helpers command. He has become one able to make withdrawals from the Heavenly vault to make new things appear on the earthly plane.

The spiritual helpers are there to provide roadside service as well as other needed help so that the faithful that is in faith rest can never be stranded on the way again. The helpers maintain, harvest and pack the fruits of his labor in the twinkling of an eye so to say for time seemingly appears to become compressed for the faithful in faith rest. Time indeed appears to stand still for the man that can do a lot in little time. This is because in regeneration God pre-positions the building blocks needed to build the new life ordained for the believer through spiritual helpers. Such will find the seeds of the things that he needs for his fulfillment available and made affordable to him. He is one that has come to the parkway of life where the way is made expedient for the faithful. It is on this parkway during regeneration, that the hills are made low, the valleys filled and the crooked made straight under the sunshine of divine love.

God knows the earthly state of all who are in faith-rest and wants to show every son that he is much beloved. Therefore the Heavenly Father readily displays his power through them. He wants to show the sons that the world is indeed his creation. He that has come into faith-rest has come into the place of favors and must affirm this truth by modeling his life after Christ. He must speak and live as the son of Heaven that he has become. Every son of Heaven is a copy of Christ Jesus in his inner man. The Christ 'borne' within each son of Heaven is not readily known for many are spiritually blind and dim of soul to perceive. But Truth cannot be buried for he that is alive in every son of Heaven comes to be known in due time. The burial bandages of Lazarus take some time to be un-wrapped. As the bandages are progressively un-wrapped, the fullness of what God has wrought in each son and purposed for him becomes more evident. All who truly seek after Christ will come to know and embrace the sons for they are permeated with the essence of the Divine. All who are not spiritually 'blind' will see that the handiworks of the sons glow with purity and that divine glory shrouds them.

The handiworks of the faithful in faith-rest are like honeycombs that showcase and bring the wisdom of the Divine into display before mankind. All such handiworks are modules which fit together into a grand whole that embodies the sustainable, fulfilling and enduring. The totality of such handiworks paints a glorious picture that unfolds with the passage of time. The honeycomb is the product of cross-pollination and blending of many parts into one pleasant whole. He that can produce the honeycomb will raise many fruitful trees. He will always have the veil of the hidden parted for him. The hidden truths are seminal seeds for the advent age of the new heaven on earth. He that is privy to them has become connected to the Divine mind and chosen to help shape the future of the earth in the similitude of Heaven. He that is so connected lives in God even as the Heavenly Father lives in him to have charity govern all his actions.

Charity is the universal umbrella that covers the faithful believer in faith-rest as he carries out his calling on earth. Charity is a strong advocate for justification before God. It leads mankind to live so that others may come to learn about the divine way. God favors the charitable in spirit and makes necessary pre-arrangements to uphold such in the work ordained ahead for them on earth. He that is in faith-rest never walks in blindness but rather is willing to tarry for Divine guidance in all endeavors. Such never forgets that he no longer labors by his own flesh but in the spirit of the living God. For him patience is not only a virtue but highly necessary. The faithful in faith rest walks under divine sunshine and so must maintain what he has received in truth, humility and thanksgiving to God. He must nurture and use his gifts well for he has been received into the company of exalted souls. He is called to maintain the 'vehicle' that he has received so that it must remain ever ready as needed for he has embarked on a great journey in service of God and humanity.

The vehicle powered by divine sunshine is not limited but universal. It can go any and everywhere as duty calls and love urges. It is the vehicle of the purified soul riding on the Divine Spirit. It can travel to wherever needed in the light of Truth and instant of time. Therefore such must not be concerned with the worldly but with serving the Heavenly Father's will for which he has been prepared. The worldly embody the weighty and encumbering which are dead weights that ground the vehicle and limit its readiness to serve. Grounding the vehicle defeats its universal purpose for then the faithful believer can no longer do all things through Christ as he has been empowered to. In that case, the believer that should have been free to soar freely among the exalted becomes a 'groundhog' trapped in the futile dreariness of an endless loop. Therefore it must be strongly emphasized that the vehicle of 'the purified soul that rides on the divine wind' given to the faithful under divine sunshine must always be maintained for good service by using it wisely and charitably to make humanity better.

The snapshot of the purified soul that rides on the divine wind taken through the lens of the world often shows one who is not easily categorized. He does not belong anywhere completely yet he belongs everywhere in part. The world may see him as incomplete yet he does not lack in any area of life. He is a Samaritan for he is not of one stock but a hybrid of various parts. He is of the circumcision and not of the concision. His circumcision is of the heart and not of the flesh. It is worth pointing out that it is the Samaritan who gets the Truth and ends up on the path of righteousness. It is the Samaritan who will offer up thanks when others will not and who will perceive Christ when many cannot or will not.

He that is seemingly out of place in this world is oftentimes the one whose works are well received by God. Such is like the Samaritan who gets intimated with the wisdom that God is a spirit that must be worshipped in spirit and truth only. Such is like the Samaritan who gets to be intimated with the knowledge that God does not care for ancestry, pedigree or grand cathedrals of worship but seeks after the heart of mankind. Such like the Samaritan will labor in the last days to bring in the last harvests of the souls of men. Such like the Samaritan labors in the spirit of true charity to bind up the wounds of the robbed bypassed by the world. Such like the Samaritan is an outsider in the world but an insider with God given to find life's true treasure by his relationship with the Divine which affords him his heart's desires. Such treasure is the kind that the world cannot take away or thieves steal but availed only when the heart is pure so that mankind can 'see' God.

Only he that is pure of heart can 'see' God. He is not seen in the flesh as men see others. God is everywhere and cannot be localized. Things seen with the eyes of the flesh are localized and therefore limited. God cannot be seen in a location but he can be known. He is known by the spirit and seen through the works of his hand. He is known when he pulses through his chosen ones to inspire feats of creative wonder. He is known when he speaks of things yet to come through the faithful. He is known in the still small voice heard through the ear of the heart in the quiet moments of life. He is known as he hears the cries and responds to the petitions of the faithful. He that can 'see' God is called to lead a kind and peaceable life. He must have compassion for the blindness of those who cannot yet 'see' as he does. He that can 'see' God in wisdom's light is no longer of the kindred of men but of Divinity. He can declare with bold certainty that Jesus Christ is indeed the son of God because he knows it to be true in his heart. He has come to know because he believed, followed and has met up with Christ in the way. The footsteps of Christ have led him to the knowledge of the Father and to share in the gifts reserved for those who live in God even as the Almighty lives in them.

There is always the residue of the flesh that attempts to inhibit the work of the spirit. The spirit is always willing but the flesh is often times weak. It is the heart of man that God seeks after and not his flesh. The heart of the true believer is without guile and purified in Truth. It is duly prepared to be an altar lit with the flame of love. Such is a heart that will always be obedient to the will of God for his desire in life is to please the Heavenly Father. The content of such a heart will be filled with the knowledge and wisdom that lead mankind to realize the fullness of divine riches availed through Christ. The possessor of such a heart is a faithful son whose ways and deeds will remain ever justified before God.

On the contrary, God rejects hearts that are ugly. Spiritual ugliness defines that which appears to be good on the outside but is dark within. The ugly heart engages only in self-serving endeavors orchestrated to earn the accolades and favor of men. The possessors of such are often praised by men who are not able to perceive or know the true contents and intentions of the heart. These hypocrites have perfected the appearance of spirituality and do excel at it. There are purveyors of the leaven of the Pharisees. The ugly heart is devoid of grace and has no share in the commonwealth of Christ. Such is filled with iniquity and wickedness. Iniquity does not use the same standards to make judgments or dispense favors. Iniquity is the inability to see all men as God's creatures for it discriminates and selects. Iniquity spawns the wicked heart which engenders the sacrifice of Truth. The wicked heart disregards conscience to take undue and unfair advantage of others. Both iniquity and wickedness constitute the antithesis of the golden rule which mandates that each man should treat his fellow man as he himself would like to be treated. The ugly heart may fool men for a season but God is never fooled for the handiworks of mankind show up in time to bear witness to the seed within him.

Chapter Notes

- ✓ The believer does not begin his spiritual journey full of faith and confident in the promises of God.
- ✓ The matured in spirit must set his mind on things above so that he can project the heavenly on earth.
- ✓ Life becomes less taxing and more expedient when earthly projects serve God's purposes.
- ✓ The faithful is like a 'bee' that uses the sunshine of God's love to propagate new life among humanity.
- ✓ The faithful in faith-rest labors not alone for he has been received into a company of spiritual helpers.
- ✓ The faithful that has come to the parkway of life will have healing and restoration effected in his life.
- ✓ The new-man born within the faithful is not readily known in the beginning but shines in due season.
- ✓ The new vehicle given to the faithful is that of his soul riding on wings of the divine Spirit.
- ✓ The sons of God do not belong anywhere completely but belong everywhere in part.
- ✓ God's power works in the sons to inspire feats of creative wonders and evoke sprinkles of wisdom.
- ✓ Spiritual ugliness defines that which appears good on the outside but is evil within.

Contents of faithful hearts are filled

With wisdom and timely knowledge

Such by divine command duly realize

Fulfilling gifts that love avails in time

Chapter 8

IN DIVINE IMMUNITY

When a believer's heart has been chosen by God as a dwelling place such becomes content to dwell in a 'small corner of the housetop' so his eyes can remain focused above. To dwell in a corner of the housetop is to be willing to live a meek and quiet life in godly consciousness. It is to live without the distractions and contention posed by the worldly minded who may even be within one's own household. He that dwells on that spiritual housetop knows that God's eye rests on him both for protection and provision. As a result, his spirit eases into that certain peace which passes understanding to enable him walk on the high road of life. The highroad of life is the parkway of the Divine where the believer's footsteps are guided by the spirit of the living God. It is a purpose-driven life lived in gentleness, great hope and blessed quietness. It is life marked by voluntary humility. It is life lived effacingly so that the spirit within remains ascendant to have full sway always. It is life lived by thinking kingly thoughts and taking heavenly steps on earth.

The spirit-led and well-purposed life is one that does not seek a stage or platform. It is life lived with work done so that graceful beauty may adorn the believer to make him twinkle from within. It is work done and sacrifices made far from the glare of the floodlight of public adulation. The stars are not those over whom the world fawns but those who bear God's precious seeds and labor to plant them on earth as needed. Though they may labor in relative obscurity and often times with tears yet they always reap in joy for the Heavenly Father unfailingly blesses their endeavors. Such are the humble souls on whom the countenance of God shines and given to twinkle as exalted stars of the lofty heights. Each star that twinkles in this way is one of God's infinite eyes planted among humanity. Each star that twinkles in this way does so for the benefit of humanity and not for self.

He that truly loves God in his heart will also love Christ for both are inseparably bonded in spirit. The way of Christ is universal and all-embracing for it seeks only to please God through the love of Truth and in light. The feeding trough of Truth and the table of enlightenment availed through Christ have ample room for everyone. But each man that aspires for such must believe enough to fear God, love truth and his fellow man also. Christ occupies the vestibule or the reception area into the heavenly mansion. No one can 'see' the Father unless he 'sees' the son first. Christ is the son that cannot be separated from the Father for both are bonded in love. The mind and will of the Father is reflected in the sons who live to serve and please him. Wherever the heart goes, the mind is bound to follow. He who has living Truth stored in heart, to live by and share faithfully with others will be transformed in spirit to meet up with the Divine in due time.

Full spiritual transformation takes more than seventeen years of faithful living in the light of truth and love through Christ. It is a journey of hope that prepares and lifts the spirit of the faithful towards that of the Father. Along the way, the traveler is gradually but steadily weaned away from the addiction of worldliness to be lifted into the realm of the free in spirit. It is a process where the believer starts as base mortal man and ends up as a purified immortal son of God after the transformation has been completed. He that is completely transformed in spirit has overcome the world. This is the noble gift that Christ Jesus gives to mankind in that he showed the way to escape the entrapment of the worldly and join the ranks of divinity. He is the one through whom the willing can learn how to take that leap of faith that enables mankind to join in spirit and be in communion with God. It is the giant leap of faith that takes mankind beyond self to find the new and better longed for. It is the only way for mankind to complete the journey that he began from the salty swamps ages ago and now through the earthly experience to hopefully end up in the heavenly home above. Sadly for humanity, only a few dare to take that leap of faith to find the true home above sorely missed deep within by all.

The faithful believer whose heart has been transformed to reflect that of Christ becomes a son of mercy given to have compassion for humanity's weaknesses. He knows that many are spiritually blind and have in most cases been unwarily misguided. Christ overlooks the outer man but seeks to bring healing to the inner man. He can feel the pain, sorrows, fears, disappointments, despair as well as the joys and hope within each man. He knows where each hurts and what each lacks. The outer man is a shell and an adornment of flesh. The inner man is the true person much sought after for it can be transformed from the moribund to the divine. He in whom the inner man is dead can never be righteous in the eye of God regardless of his accomplishments in the world.

Righteousness comes from the ability to hear and obey God's commands. The true believer hears with the ear of the heart and sees with the eye of the spirit. The dead in spirit is deaf as well as blind and consequently cannot hear or perceive the Divine. He that can hear with the heart and perceive with the spirit is led into greater love. The dead in spirit can never know greater love for he has not loved God as he should have. By the embrace of Truth through Christ, the dead in spirit can come to know Divine love. He that has come to know God's love cannot help but love Christ. To love God is to love Christ and vice versa. By the same token to know Christ is to know God. It is for this reason that God bestows his righteousness on the faithful who walks in the truth, light and love of Christ. Such is one who cannot help but be covered in the warmth of Divine love. The heart that loves God is able to hear his commands. Such a heart loves to obey God's commands for he knows that there are profitable and will do him much good in the end. The commands of God are love impulses received through the antennae of the spirit that cause no grief but yield much benefit in life.

The faithful that truly loves and fears God will be transformed in due season for the Heavenly Father cannot reject the love that is sincere. It is not possible for God to do so for he is love. Such who love God sincerely will be lifted up in spirit to overcome the world. They will be protected from the wiles and traps of the prince of the darkness of this world in their earthly passage. They will pass through the miry clay and minefields of the world unscathed. Even when they encounter pitfalls, the love of God will show them a way out of it. When they stumble, the love of God will help to lift them up. It is by such love availed through the gifts of grace and mercy that God affords protection to the faithful. The love of God immunizes the faithful in the certainty of godliness that the evil in the world cannot touch. All who are immunized in godliness receive from the heavenly table to share in love with those willing to embrace Truth.

He that is immunized in godliness is an exalted soul given to replant the earth in the manner of heaven. He is part of God's victorious army that has triumphed over darkness.

He is the faithful who has wielded the sword of truth nobly to be equipped with the silver bullets required for victory in every sphere of life. Goodness and mercy follow the immunized in godliness for his spirit has found everlasting habitation in the Divine. He is the culmination of the unyielding love and ceaseless impulses that work to rescue God's favorite creation man from the grips of the prince of darkness bent on destroying all that is good.

For many the damage to the soul inflicted by a sinful life is irreparable but for some there is hope. The enemy of light is subtle in his destructive ways and attempts to conceal the damage so that it is not readily obvious. He is the crafty and wily one who is surreptitious in all his ways. The damage that he inflicts on humanity appears over time as degradation, decay and death set in. In feeding the flesh rather than the spirit, the faithless fail and abdicate their roles as the divinely appointed caretakers of God's creation. It is for this reason that the earth and humanity teeters on the edge of a precipitous abyss. Yet it remains God's grand vision to rescue the willing from looming catastrophe and use such as foundation for a new beginning.

God loves man too much and has been patiently transforming the willing from the base into the purified in spirit. These faithful ones are being transformed into the spiritual clones of Christ Jesus. The latter is the first fruit of this spiritual transformation. The seeds of that first fruit have been used by God to produce more fruits of the same kind down through the ages to the present time. The Heavenly Father has prepared, readied and positioned these 'Christ-Men' all over the world to become the impetus for recreating the earth in the order of heaven. Most would agree that at the present time, the world is indeed a dark and evil place. They would also agree that the old ways do not work and that a global catastrophe is imminent if the present trend continues and nothing changes.

Without a doubt, this present age of the earth is on its last leg and has just about run its course. There is a new age set to replace the present one that looms on the horizon. Most of humanity will not be part of the new creation except for the transformed in spirit that have been chosen and prepared to be its foundational seedlings. The chosen are already living under the law of glorious liberty of the spirit of life through Christ as the sons of Heaven. The glory of God is being shed on those that are chosen as God uses them to produce marvelous works all over the earth. These sons have the freedom to ask what they wish from the Heavenly Father. They are on the divine speed-dial list for each son has the ear of God who has their ears as well. God will answer when they call home to him through prayers. They in turn never fail to carry out his Divine wishes on earth as he makes such known to them.

Each son of Heaven hears with the ear of the heart and is

given to obey the will of the Heavenly Father. Therefore each has the 'carte blanche' to petition for anything but he must let the criteria of truth, purity, honesty, justice, loveliness and goodness govern all that he aspires for. It is these criteria that impart virtue and life to the handiworks of mankind. He that lives under the glorious law of liberty must be diligent to work night and day for he has been equipped to do the amazing in timely order. All things become sustainable, fulfilling and enduring in the new age for eternity is the order of the day in the regime of light. The ever-lasting reach out and are linked with each other in an inseparable web of new life. Each feeds the others and the others feed it in a cycle of sustainability within a commonwealth of the pure. Such is the nature of things when spirits commune in the highest order for it becomes a feast of love laid out to the everlasting tune of divine glory in subtle tones evoked by a golden sunshine.

Chapter Notes

- ✓ The spirit of the faithful that lives in voluntary humility will have full sway over the flesh.
- ✓ The purposed and spirit-led life in Christ does not seek a stage or platform in order to be noticed.
- ✓ The table of enlightenment affords nourishment for those that fear God, love truth and humanity.
- ✓ The journey of faith is one of hope that prepares and lifts the spirit of the faithful towards Heaven.
- ✓ The commands of God are the impulses of a loving and caring father who hopes for the best for all.
- ✓ The faithful that loves and fears God passes through the miry clay and minefields unscathed.
- ✓ The unyielding and unceasing love of God seeks to rescue man from destructive impulses.
- ✓ The damage inflicted by the enemy appears over time as degradation, decay and death set in.

The spirit is that uplifting divine wind

Knows when to rise and the way to go

Same calls the faithful to ride and soar

Until the task at hand is well and done

Chapter 9

IN GLORIOUS LIBERTY

The faithful believer who has put his trust in God knows to tarry for divine guidance before making crucial decisions and taking important steps in life. Life is about making plans and facing difficult choices. It is a given fact that most things ventured in life turn out far from the expected. Sadly most things planned and hoped for are never realized. Often times the net result is different from what was desired. Therefore for the most part in life, it is not uncommon for mankind to be stuck in undesirable situations and tough predicaments on account of bad choices made. Life need not be that way for there is another way of living that the wise have come to know. The wise way is to wait for God's okay in order to be sure that the path is clear so that one can be shielded from pitfalls and disasters due to unforeseen circumstances. Even when trying circumstances and acts of nature happen, those who know to tarry for guidance can still prevail and come out of their troubles well protected.

To tarry spiritually is to rein in the flesh so that the antennae of the spirit may be fully tuned to know the Divine will. Tarrying involves meditating on God's words of Truth so as to obtain certainty and clarity of understanding while seeking guidance about life's issues. He that meditates in this wise will be given to hear, see and know from the divine source. He will always be able to translate seeds of heaven into right earthly shapes. He will be given to know the outcome of earthly endeavors beforehand.

The faithful believer who has learned to put his trust in God will prevail through all of life's circumstances. Such a believer who puts his trust in God fully has made him the sovereign Lord of his life. It does take some time to really let go and let God take complete control. The decision to let God have total control is the beast of Ephesus that many are not able to overcome. However the faithful believer soon learns that he can never do better by leaning on his own understanding. He soon figures out from experience that it turns out to be much better for him in the end to let God direct his steps. It is when the believer is certain in this knowledge that he becomes willing to let God be the sovereign guide of his life. Only then will he be willing to be ready at the Lord's command to be used as the need arises. Those that live for God's purposes in this way under the guidance of his Divine light are such that are shielded to abound in goodness in life.

The spirit of God is like the wind in that it chooses when to rise and the direction to head. In other words, it takes the spirit of God to initiate and govern the course of action in the believer's life. It works much like the electrical current that flows through and powers a piece of equipment. The faithful believer is like a piece of equipment reconditioned by Divine will that needs the flow of the spirit to accomplish each intended purpose. The faithful must yield when the spirit rises for it will lift him up to a greater height than he can rise on his own. He must hold out his wings of faith and glide along in glorious liberty as the spirit leads him. The divine wind does not rise without occasion. It comes so that a certain task can be accomplished. The faithful who has learned to soar on the wings of faith must ride the divine wind until the task initiated is completed.

The faithful is called at the Lord's command to ride the divine wind to accomplish his earthly endeavors. Such is given a companion ordained by God as a partner through life's journey. The faithful that rides the divine wind leads the effort and his companion complements those efforts so that God's purposes are fulfilled. The companion may seem ill-suited for the role at first glance but looks will be deceiving in this case. The companion will have glaring faults and imperfections when seen with the eyes of the flesh. But God sees with the eye of spirit and uses the seemingly ill-suited to confound the wise of the world. Divine wisdom and power will come to be manifested not only through the rider of the Divine wind but through his companion as well. The companion that seems so ill-suited soon turns out to be the best person for the job indeed. Such will turn out to be the best companion to enable God's purposes to be well and fully served by the rider of the divine wind.

Although the soul that has been chosen to ride the divine wind will be afforded a companion with seemingly obvious faults and imperfections yet she will show forth many hidden attributes over time. Each hidden attribute will be revealed and offered up in due season as needed to complement the efforts of the rider of the Divine wind. The companion is vital in the life of the faithful servant of God. If the latter can be visualized as a piece of electrical equipment, then the companion is the protective cover that shrouds it. The cover shelters the equipment from the earthly elements in all kinds of weather so that the equipment can remain ready for work as called upon. The companion is spiritually joined to the rider of the divine wind as a faithful laborer divinely appointed to assist in carrying out the earthly labors ordained for him and will suffice for those endeavors. The wind rider is charged not to find faults but to constantly pray for wisdom on how to bring out the best from what God has afforded him. The Heavenly Father foresees everything and has things figured out in the best interests of all those that serve him faithfully in love.

The rider of the Divine wind is a chosen vessel and water-bearer for all times and seasons. He is the incubating nursery for faith who together with the companion labors so that the future may be secured and abound in good fruits. He is the host of the good things buried within that are only revealed in the fullness of time. He is the digger of wells who holds the key to the fountain for he only knows where and how to dig for the water of life when others do not. He is one given to call up the water buried deep so that life may abound on earth. He brings out things that are new but old. He rediscovers that which has been lost and forgotten as he awakens the dormant things to life to make places come to life again. Yet he does all that peaceably with the quietness borne of an innate understanding and intimate bond with the Heavenly Father. Therefore, he will not fight but trusts in the goodness of Providence to take care of his needs.

But the well digger is a solitary traveler on the road of life who travels not in the company of men but in the company of spiritual messengers. Often he finds the noise of the world to be disquieting, pestering and distractive for it obscures the still small voice that he yearns to hear. It takes a life of blessed quietness borne of meditation and seeking time alone with God to be a worthy servant through faith. Nevertheless he who digs the well must have someone to draw out the water or his labors will be for naught. It is for this reason that God makes provision for an earthly companion to meet this need so that all who thirst can taste living water.

The rider of the Divine wind who serves faithfully will have the anointing of God on him as a proxy of the Heavenly Father on earth. He will prevail over all that he encounters for he is immunized in godliness through Truth and will always find escape from the traps of the prince of the darkness of this world. He that faithfully serves in this wise is very much like a white pebble which has been washed and purified by the words of Truth to become a divine point of contact amidst a sea of dark pebbles. Such is a lover of Truth who is truthful in all things and at all times. He who loves Truth will hate the ways of the world. Therefore he who loves Truth will be hated by the world. The world may not but the Heavenly Father will love him beyond measure.

Truth is the element that bonds every faithful servant with the Divine. God is a spirit and they that worship him must worship him in Spirit and Truth. God cannot be seen with the eyes of the flesh but he can be known by those who always speak Truth in love regardless of cost. The lover of Truth will meet up with Christ sooner than later. Only those who love Truth will understand the gift that Christ brings to mankind. Christ is revealed to those who speak and love Truth. The lover of Truth already lives life in accordance with the golden rule. He will not cut corners or take short cuts in his dealings with humanity but seek to travel on the path of righteousness. Truth is the language spoken by those who have been set free to soar in spirit to the exalted heights to live in glorious liberty.

Truth is the ingredient which affords the faithful believer glimpses into the hidden things of God and makes him to shine in light in a world of darkness. Truth must never be compromised by the believer that seeks to know God. Lies keep the Divine spirit away to keep mankind earth-bound. The believer that serves God faithfully must guard his tongue always and learn to speak only the few words of truth necessary to get his point across. He must cultivate the quiet and peaceable life. He must avoid making too many promises and overly committing himself for his word is his bond with the Heavenly Father. He must constantly pray for wisdom so that he may speak with grace always to the glory of God for in his words lie the power to make life or death abound.

The believer who lives by Truth models an exemplary life for he lives above the way of the world. He that speaks Truth easily recognizes that which is not true. The ways and sounds of Truth are familiar to him. Therefore when that which is not true comes along his way it sounds out of tune and appears out of place for lies just do not fit well with him. Truth registers a definitive note in the ear of the spirit and leaves a memorable imprint on the hearts of men. Truth does not seek to impress nor does it seek to be liked. It only seeks to remove the clutter so that the core can be free to shine. Truth is the food of the spirit of life for it nourishes and sustains the starving soul to bring it back to new life. Truth avails the needed uplift so that the spirit of the believer can flourish to rise above the world.

Truth is buoyant and takes the faithful man to places beyond his flesh. Such a man is no longer boxed in within himself as other men are for he has been freed from his earthly shackles. The free in spirit must therefore learn to live victoriously in the glorious liberty which Truth has afforded him. He can get to the place close to the heart of God reserved for a special few where much can be known and obtained through Divine Providence. The free in spirit must serve humanity in true Charity so that thereby he can change the world for better. To do otherwise is to risk becoming a fallen star. The latter is the unworthy that has used God's gifts for his own gain. Such will never awaken to the full image of God for he will never be completely transformed to Christ. He will not remain as the starry but return to the earthy and weighty. He will never receive the eternal crown of glory for he has failed to live according to the law of glorious liberty. He has not overcome the world for his soul has not broken free from the earth. The world has overcome him.

- ✓ The believer who has put his trust in God tarries for divine guidance before making decisions in life.
- ✓ The faithful know that they do better when God is involved than relying on own understanding.
- ✓ The faithful can be likened to equipment powered by the Divine to accomplish intended purposes.
- ✓ The faithful laborer is given a companion that seems ill-suited but turns out to be best for the job.
- ✓ Tarrying for guidance to obtain clarity about life's issues works as a divine fail-safe.
- ✓ The faithful live in peace and quietness due to an innate understanding and intimacy with the Divine.
- ✓ Truth is the ingredient that affords the faithful believer knowledge that is hidden to the faithless.
- ✓ Truth registers a definitive note in the spirit and leaves a memorable imprint on the hearts of men.
- ✓ The free in spirit must learn to live victoriously in the glorious liberty which has been afforded him.

To hold on to the traditions of the past

When mankind has a foretaste of the new

Precludes him from ascension to the place

Where Heaven has ordered a feast of love

Chapter 10

PERFECTION IN THE SUM

There is a clearly spelt out warning in the Holy Scriptures that implores mankind to be careful not to mock God. Regrettably, this warning which needs to be taken seriously by humanity is mostly treated with disregard by many. Although it has been pointed out countless times that it is not possible to deceive God yet mankind refuses to heed this warning on account of spiritual blindness. Man mocks God in many different ways some obvious and others concealed. The disparaging of scriptures and the blatant disregard for God's commandments is one way. But a more insidious but no less spiteful way is spiritual hypocrisy. Many know and talk about what God requires of mankind but sadly are not able to live as they profess. As a result, religion abounds in many shapes, forms and congregations yet a spiritual famine besets humanity. Evil and wickedness reign in the hearts of many. The young are discouraged by the hypocrisy and injustice of it all. The Heavenly Father who sees and knows all is aware of this travesty of the times. This state of affairs surely breaks his heart without measure and has taken his long suffering patience to the extreme. By mankind's acts of willful disobedience, God's wearied hand of inevitable justice cannot be stayed much longer as mankind has opened the door of doom to his shame and sad regret.

Another subtle but no less harmful way that mankind mocks God is by his persistent and consummate desire to sow in the flesh instead of the spirit. Mankind has become overly enamored with the material. He is not able to understand that man reaps as he sows. Wisdom clearly cautions that he who sows in the flesh reaps corruption but he that sows in the spirit reaps life. The lust for the material leads mankind to cut corners, seek short cuts and compromise Truth. The lust for earthly materials keeps man's soul in bondage and leads him to spiritual death eventually. The soul purified in Truth is lifted up so the spirit can rejoin the source of life from whence it sprang forth. But the soul that is in bondage wallows in the miry clay of the earth and will never rise for lack of life in the spirit. It will remain listless and hunger forever for life but will not find. The Heavenly Father is the source of life. Man's earthly journey becomes meaningless if he is not able to reconcile with the Divine and find everlasting life before his time on earth runs out.

The believer who heeds the teachings of Christ Jesus will grow in knowledge to where his spirit is able to break free of the shackling hold of the earth. His soul will be freed of the bondage of the earth. He will come to reap new life within the divine fold. He will morph into a new creature borne in godliness that lives a spirit led-life more and a flesh driven life less. He will become a spirit-man borne from the old self of his flesh-man. He who continues to sow in the spirit will continue to grow closer to the heart of God. He will gradually be remade in spirit into the full image of his Maker so that it can be said for a fact that he has come home. The reason for the creation of the earth by God is so that it can be used as a nursery for the souls of men. He that is willing to accept 'the garment of the lamb of sacrifice' as his earthly cloak will be gradually remade in the image of the Divine from the base material of his old self. He that has been remade in that image will be able to eat figs from the tree of life and thereby come into knowledge needed for the times.

Man's time on earth should really be about being remade in the spiritual image of the Divine. All the situations and places that the faithful believer goes through in life sum up into the process of remaking him in that light. He that has completed this remaking process will begin to walk on earth under the cloak of Divinity. It is a process of initiation into eternal life and the all-knowing wisdom of God. It is for this reason that Christ Jesus came so that he can model the process for those that believe in him. Anyone that truly follows in the path laid down by Christ Jesus to complete the process will become a 'Christ-Man' who can model the way as well for others who aspire.

During the transformational process a lot of 'pruning' of the worldly takes place in the life of the believer through the unseen hand of God. During those years of spiritual transformation the aspiring believer learns to yield and accept Divine will as the sovereign guide of life. While this takes place, he will be gradually weaned away from the encumbering ways of the world. Those things that are pruned and that he is weaned away from are the unnecessary that inhibit spiritual growth. Those are the weeds which invade the garden of the mind to clutter the soul with wantonness. On the other hand, the seed of life is Truth taught and learned through spiritual experiences in faithfully following after Christ.

Spiritual transformation can be viewed as a distillation process in which the weighty and earthly material sink to the bottom but the light and starry material rise to the top. The weighty material that sinks to the bottom and gets jettisoned is due to the old nature. The light material that rises to the top is borne of the new self through the light of Christ. Only the very important as well as faith in God's goodness are needed for transformation because the path leads upwards where the weighty things impede progress. It is a path of amazement that winds upwards in divinely ordered steps. The believer must trust that God is in control and knows what he is doing. The journey serves to peel away the wrappings of the ego, correct the misguidance of the past and reverse the ravages of time for the faithful. Only the essential core of the spirit remains at the end of spiritual transformation. The core of the spirit is what God is looking for in mankind and that by which he sheds his glory on the faithful. Within that core lies the purified soul of man in which is found the kernel of the Divine. The latter is what God hid in man in the first place and what he comes looking for in the end. It is this kernel which embodies the connection between man the creature and God his Creator.

The more that the believer is purified in spirit is the more that he becomes aware of the reality of God in everything and everywhere. He is in effect getting closer to the source of all knowledge and wisdom in spirit. He is being initiated into a greater understanding where he will begin to understand the universal language of creation. Such a believer will come into a greater and better understanding of what all things in nature are communicating to each other. He is able then to discern all things and nothing of importance can be hidden from him. He is conscious both of the local and the universal issues that pertain to life as one in spiritual communion with the Divine. In effect, he has become a citizen of the universe who lives to serve God more and himself less. He has become a son of Heaven who walks among men under the mantle of divinity. His lot in life then becomes to serve God's will and thereby fulfill his divine purposes on earth.

Those who are reconnected in spirit with the Divine are the proxy through whom God interfaces with humanity.

None others can suffice for this duty except those fully matured in the spirit of Christ. Such hearts are the only ones acceptable to the heavenly Father as points of contact with mankind. These are the true temples of God who as universal spirits look for the things that unite humanity and not such that separate mankind. There is no division and distinction in Christ for his body is a commonwealth of co-sharers. Christ is perfected in the sum of the imperfect parts when and where the veil of darkness has been chased away by the dawn of light. If the different parts are not assembled to fit together, then there is no vehicle to be powered by the Divine. The different parts can never be made to fit perfectly where darkness still exists but only in the pure and true light of God through Christ.

There is but one tradition that all who truly live in Christ observe. The latter are the golden in spirit who come from different backgrounds, cultures and traditions. Such are the faithful ones who have found Christ through living by the golden rule. They seek not after glory for self but after the glory of God through Christ. Such that live by this higher law defy the traditions of men. The traditions of men are borne from that which was fostered at Babel. The traditions of men serve to separate mankind. Traditions are from the past and becloud the eye of the spirit to keep the truth veiled for many. They embody the serpentine that often seduces and beguiles the ignorant into darkness and spiritual demise. He that holds on to the traditions of the past, when he has known the new, will not be able to come up to the feast of love through Christ for he seeks to patch the new on to the old. His spirit will not be fully awakened to be joined to the eternal stream of the Divine.

He that has been bestowed with a universal spirit has left the old ways. Abraham, the father of faith, left the old ways of the old country to begin his journey of faith to a new and far away land. He had not known that land beforehand but the spirit of God led him there regardless. He was not led there in a sprint but in a deliberate and measured way. It had to be that way in order to give him time to break away from the old ways. God takes time to reconfigure the faithful believer in the universal way through patience, obedience and sacrifice. The believer that has the universal spirit is received everywhere. The faithful that has the universal spirit has received the passport that lets him in anywhere. He must watch out for the traps of mankind's traditions and ceremonies. Although these are often times cleverly disguised so as not to appear to be so, there are designed to cater to man's desire to 'make' himself a master and be more than he is. The ways of tradition are designed to make men gloat in their own prowess so others can fawn over them. For man to presume to be a master in the world above others is an ill-conceived and misguided notion. God is the Master of all and those who aspire to be justified before him must live by the heavenly way of the golden rule where all are brethren in the light of Truth and love as God's children.

God is man's Creator and Master. Man has a daunting challenge in attempting to master self by his own devices. It is faith in God that settles the score of life. The man that aspires for mastery in life must rise above the world and go beyond self into the glorious liberty of true light availed through Christ. Only in the reflection of true light can one know true self and thereby come to know his Maker. Once exalted there, he must live to serve God's will and purposes as a co-regent with all the other sons of heaven. It is only through the ladder of faith in God and belief in Christ that the true self can be known to be mastered. He who builds must do so on the sure foundation of Christ. Building on the traditions and ceremonies of man is like building on the quick sands of time as the so-called great civilizations of the past attest. Traditions and ceremonies choose the wisdom of man instead of searching out the true wisdom of God. God's wisdom is ever unfolding, fresh and enduring but man's wisdom becomes stale soon enough. Traditions and ceremonies are devised to praise man the creature instead of God the Creator.

The faithful who can soar to live in glorious liberty is never to be weary in well doing. He must continue in well doing as led in spirit for such works are well received by God and count as treasure stored in the heavenly vaults. Such are works that serve as the seeds of goodness planted for future harvest. The works initiated and enabled by the spirit of God are enduring works that produce good fruits. Such are to be copied and passed on so that the benefits inherent in them can reach all. It makes sense and bodes well for mankind to plant seeds of the Divine with his limited time on earth. The good labor carried out for God and goodness is the only endeavor that will endure in the end when it counts most. On the contrary, the works and labors dictated by the flesh result in dead works. Since dead works are not governed by the spirit but by the flesh, they have no inherent life and so do not endure. Rather such engender envy and contention at the very least. They may look good to the eye in the beginning but fade away sooner or later. They may smell of success for a time but not for long as all things borne of the flesh tend towards decay. At the end, every dead work is just an invitation for maggots to come to feast.

The believer that lives in glorious liberty no longer cares for the works of the flesh. The latter defile and weigh down the soul so that the spirit cannot take flight readily. He that lives in glorious liberty does everything as led in spirit for he has ceased from the works of the flesh. Rather he lives to serve mankind with love and pureness of heart for by such do humanity come to be exalted. He that is led in his endeavors by the Divine is a bearer of precious seeds. He must be firm in spirit so as to remain an acceptable and worthy vessel for use by God. The flesh tends to rear its ugly head occasionally so as to detract the faithful. He that aims to serve God well must let go of many things in order to stay above the world's fray and remain indefatigable in carrying out the work ordained for him. It requires repetitive effort to overcome the pockets of entrenched resistance in the hearts of men. It takes time and diligence to overcome the evil ways of darkness in the world. It is not an easy job with a quick fix but that which must be done with patience, understanding, forgiveness and love.

To convert mankind from the sinful ways of the world is to battle the enemy for the soul of the sinner. It is an exhausting effort that taxes mind, body and spirit. The standard bearer for God must be strong in spirit and fit in body. He must be equipped and geared up for battle at all times. The spread of the kingdom of God happens gradually but steadily. The effective warrior for God must hold his flesh in check in order to be victorious in his battles. He that is called to serve God must live the life of the good shepherd who denies himself so that the beloved flock may abound. He that is a good shepherd often carries deep wounds inflicted by the enemy on account of his faith in God, belief in Christ and love for the flock. But these are only wounds of the flesh for nothing can touch him that has become divine in spirit.

Chapter Notes

- ✓ Most have an understanding of what God requires of mankind but choose not to live as they know.
- ✓ Mankind's earthly journey becomes meaningless if he is not able to reconcile with God.
- ✓ The faithful that willingly puts on 'the garment of sacrifice' will be duly remade in divine image.
- ✓ Spiritual transformation winds upwards and eschews the material for such drag down.
- ✓ Greater enlightenment affords an understanding of the universal issues pertaining to life.
- ✓ The sons are universal spirits who propagate those things that unite mankind in light and love.
- ✓ The kindness of the golden rule is the one tradition that those who live by divine light observe.
- ✓ The Divine guides the believer in measured steps to afford him time to break away from the old ways.
- ✓ The faithful that seeks to rise into glorious liberty must learn to master the way through Christ.
- ✓ God's standard bearer must be strong in mind, body and spirit so as to be ready for battle always.
- ✓ The good shepherd carries deep wounds as the mark of faithfulness and abiding love.

A gift to one's self counts for nothing

As it seeks to glorify the imperfect self

But a gift to others in selfless sacrifice

Is perfection realized by the imperfect

Chapter 11

A CLEFT IN THE ROCK

The elect is he that has been chosen by the Heavenly Father to be his proxy on earth for the people. He that God chooses is usually led through a process of spiritual transformation that takes place in life's wilderness apart from the people. God will always let the people know that such an elect one will return someday no longer as one of the people but as one divinely ordained to be a guiding light in the heavenly way for them. Sadly many among the people will not acknowledge the elect son but will rather be dismissive of him due to spiritual blindness borne of faithlessness. However those given to embrace Truth will wait for him whom the Divine took from among them to teach the exalted way for he will return in due season as a son of Hope to show them the way of light and love.

Those who wait for the return of the son of Hope will be blessed for having faith. But sadly, most will be precluded from the new light because they love their old lives too much to care for the strange new way. The faithful that wait for the return of the elect son of Hope will be spiritually nourished through grace. Such who wait are those who long for goodness and know that God never fails to fulfill his promises. The power and protection of God will extend to those that wait patiently for the son that was foretold. Those that love the elect are loved in return by the Heavenly Father. He duly rewards their patient hope and faith for they are the sheep of the flock that refused to be scattered and unto whom the good shepherd returns in due season. They are the keepers of the 'faith of the fathers' for the advent of the elect son is always pre-known and foretold. Those who wait for the return of the son of Hope know that he holds the key to all that ails the people. They know that he is that fountain of new life that will bubble up living water to assuage their parched collective souls. This knowledge is planted in the hearts able to receive by the Divine Father so that such may know to embrace the son of Hope upon return.

The son of Hope is an elect one through whom God's grace attends the people. Grace is the divine gift which affords spiritual protection and avails provision to the young that are not yet established in faith. It is like the sheltering and nurturing provision that a parent makes available to a dependent child. The parent hopes that in due time the child will grow into maturity as a man and be able to take care of self as well as others hopefully. The believer that reaches full spiritual maturity in Christ to stand on his own has grown from grace to come under the mercy. Such is is one who can ask and receive directly from God. He need not go through another to make his request known for goodness and mercy now attend him.

The sons receive spiritual gifts in mercy from the Heavenly Father but pass same forward to those willing to embrace Truth to receive as grace. In that sense grace is not only foundational but all-encompassing for it covers every believer through his spiritual journey to full maturity in Christ. The knowledge and truth which the teacher pours into his disciple is conveyed through grace and will never leave him but will become the foundation of his faith. The disciple is just a vessel to keep that which has been poured into him by the mentoring teacher. The worthy vessel that retains the contents faithfully is the extension of the source from which it receives.

It is in this wise that grace originates as mercy from God's heavenly throne to flow through Christ Jesus to reach the original apostles. It then courses through time across the branches and down the bough of the tree of faith to reach the believer of today. Grace speaks softly but reverberates assuredly within the fellowship of Christ. Grace is the foundation upon which the way of Christ rests. Without grace, the way of Christ will be washed away by life's torrents and torments. Grace abounds in those hearts where sincerity, humility and thankfulness hold counsel to delight mankind. It should be pointed out that for the believer to stand before God under mercy he has to abound in grace. Grace will flow through the one under mercy to meet the spiritual needs of those that trust and embrace Truth by him. Such under mercy is the good shepherd whose prayers of supplication on behalf of the flock will always be answered by the Heavenly Father.

Grace serves to keep the believer humble as well as remind him to be thankful for life's blessings. Grace shields and mitigates the hurt of a derisive world that mocks Truth. Grace meets and supplies the daily needs of the aspiring believer so that he is able to grow in faith. Grace reassures the believer that even though he seems to walk alone yet he is being watched over and never really alone. In short, grace is the umbrella that protects the young in faith from harmful exposure to the unhealthy and hostile elements of the world. It is not possible for the young believer to grow into maturity in Christ without grace just as it is not possible for any baby to raise himself into adulthood without the aid of parents. The young in faith has to be nurtured along the way through grace divinely availed to reach him through another. The infant in the way of Christ must be raised through grace until he can mature and be established to stand before God in mercy in accordance with divine will.

It is not mankind's flesh that is being raised in the way of Christ but the spirit within. Grace works to protect the nascent spirit within man for the flesh works to stifle spiritual growth. He that walks in humility, sincerity and thankfulness minimizes the obstruction of the flesh. He that does not do so gives his flesh free reign to inhibit the spirit. When the latter is the case the spirit within will have no chance to flourish for God resists the proud, the untruthful and the unthankful man. Pride, lies and lack of thankfulness negate grace to set it to naught. They make grace to become of no effect in nurturing the spirit within. The believer that continues in true and humble confession with due thanks to God in all things always will grow stronger in faith from infancy to full spiritual maturity in Christ. The lustful ways of his old nature will cease and be replaced by the longing of a new nature that desires to please the heavenly Father. Such a seeker is well on his way to spiritual transformation for a new person in Christ has come to life within him.

Spiritual maturity in Christ is that which defines the sons of God. The place in which the matured in spirit dwells is the realm of mercy. He that comes into the place of mercy will receive a new name for he has become known to the Heavenly Father. Such has become a son of Heaven worthy to be entrusted with the sacred and hidden. He is one that has come into harmony with the Creator and creation. As such all things in creation will begin to communicate with him for he comes in peace to bring glory to the highest in Heaven. He will have the insightful knowledge needed for every situation that he encounters for he lives to serve God's will on earth. The place of mercy should be the desired spiritual destination for it defines righteousness before God. The realm of mercy is the place close to the divine heart where the souls of the noble cluster in godliness. It is the divine household and the gathering place of all who are reborn in true light. It is the spiritual abode of those for whom God has ordained great vision and strong faith.

Those that have been received into the realm of mercy are given to ride the divine highway which leads through the high places where the earthly and heavenly meet. It is the place of the new wine and new life regenerated in Christ. It is the place where the way of God reigns supreme and those of man count for little. He that lives under mercy no longer lives under his own will but under that of the Heavenly Father. The place of mercy is a cleft in the Rock that harbors the pure of heart whose handiwork is pleasing to God. It is the place where goodness is exchanged for mercy. Money is not needed for the corruptible has no portion there. The handiworks of mercy glow in purity from within for such are borne of the pure that seeks not after the praise of men but only the best for humanity. Only the noble few who have proven worthy of grace through Christ are allowed into the realm of mercy. The Heavenly Father can trust them with the purer and greater that are reserved for only the exalted because they have proven to be worthy in the little.

Such that have come into full knowledge of God and are dedicated to serve in love so that others too may come to know as well soon become exalted for worthy service to humanity. Such who have been willing to sacrifice all for love are duly adopted by the Heavenly Father. Such see God as the Father of all mankind and other men as brethren. Such are the ones that belong to the universe for they are woven into the fabric of life and bestowed with an everlasting spirit. They alight on earth as God's gift to mankind and take flight back to their true home in Heaven when their earthly duty is done. Such touch down on earth in a brief moment of time to model the heavenly way to the ignorant and spiritually blind trapped in the lowly way of the earthen. They may walk clumsily on the face of the earth because their strength is not in their feet but in their wings. Such are lifted in spirit by their wings as they pray and can soar in spirit to places beyond man's imagination and dreams. Their earthly sacrifices are well received above as sweet smelling savor by God who readily grants their requests as they endeavor to win back lost souls from darkness into light. They are the ones on whom the greater divine light shines and to whom much is revealed as enlightened sons remade in the likeness of the Father.

Each enlightened soul has been earmarked to serve God gloriously and must learn to use the host of services available to him. The Heavenly Father will hardly deny anything to those that serve him worthily and faithfully on earth. It is not a bother for the son to ask of his father if it is in the line of the family business. All that the father has is for those who serve him well. Regrettably the sons of

Light do not know how to work that which they have. It is like an electronic device that has the functional capability to make complex computations but the user only uses it to carry out simple arithmetical operations. The son must not limit himself by wallowing with the pigs in the mud. Pigs do not fly but eagles do. He must avoid that which fouls his dreams and dulls his vision. He that has been given great vision and strong faith must carry out a heavenly task on earth each day. The bane of the sons is to under-achieve for they fail to fully use the services available to them. Each son must not be derelict so that he can take flight back to the heavenly home when the earthly duty is done. The son of glory has been prepared to carry out all that he does in the spirit of the living God and not by his own strength. He must always remember this so that he can optimize his time and maximize his potential to serve God gloriously. He must remain constantly aware of the limitless possibilities available to him and be well-positioned all times to be used as needed for God's glory.

Chapter Notes

- ✓ To keep the faith of the fathers is to wait in patient hope for the advent of the elect foretold aforetime.
- ✓ The son of Hope is a fountain of living water to assuage the collective soul of the people of God.
- ✓ The son of Hope is the elect of Heaven through whom God's attends to the people of faith.
- ✓ Grace is like an umbrella that protects the believer from exposure in an unhealthy and hostile world.
- ✓ The abode of mercy is close to the heart of God and the noble souls cluster there.
- ✓ The abode of mercy is a cleft in the Rock that harbors the pure whose works are pleasing to God.
- ✓ The 'manna' of due knowledge affords spiritual insight needed to deal with everyday issues.
- ✓ The faithful in the way is woven into the fabric of life to be bestowed with an everlasting spirit.
- ✓ The faithful that desires to be of glorious service to God must learn to master the gifts availed to him.

Ever in communion with the Divine

The gardener fit to tend the precious

Is bonded in meditation and prayers

Whether in his labors or in pleasure

Chapter 12

BORNE OF THE GOOD TREE

The epistles of the Apostle Paul serve to inspire those who aspire for spiritual transformation that leads mankind into reconciliation and intimate knowledge of God. Those letters, written purely from a place of love, also hold out hope that those who have come into that knowledge and intimacy can also influence others to seek for reconciliation with the heavenly Father as well. To win a soul from darkness to light is a very noble endeavor. There are only a few things in man's spiritual experience that can compare to the fulfillment of bearing a child in the kingdom way as a spiritual father. It is an occasion for much joy both in Heaven above and on earth below when that happens. He that has nurtured another in the way of Christ to bring him into divine light is his spiritual father for both are linked in spirit by the umbilical cord of love.

Both the Father and spiritual son have entered into that mystical bond from which all blessings flow. The bond between Father and sons provide the motivation for God to showcase his awesome power for man's benefit. The goodness and mercy that follow the Father also reaches the son that walks in true faithfulness. The bond of the father and son is the cradle of regeneration where all that wisdom has bestowed on the father is passed on to the son in love. The father is joined up with the son in an endless link where there is no end but always a new beginning. It is the saga of the good fight fought and the race finished in victory when the baton of the noble in spirit is passed on to the worthy receiver.

The example of Timothy is that of the worthy son who has grown in faith to love and hunger after the things of God. He is a son that affirms his spiritual father Paul before God for he is a good fruit produced from a worthy tree. A son such as Timothy brings much joy to the heart of the spiritual father for he has justified his progenitor's efforts and hope. He has kept and treasured in his heart those precious things which were poured into him. He is a son that has shown faithfulness in the little things so that he can be entrusted with more and greater things. Such is a son that will abound in faith, grace and wisdom. Regrettably, for that one son that proves to be worthy there are many more who prove to be unworthy in the way of Christ. Those are the ones that are overcome by worldly cares and lusts. Those are the ones who are nurtured with the word of God but fail to heed them. Therefore they lack spiritual strength to resist temptation when they encounter such. They fail the test of faith and prove to be unworthy of noble service to God.

Many who have been dutifully taught turn out to be loud professors of faith but not true confessors or faithful worshippers before God. Such worship God with words but not with the heart. However the son that proves faithful and grows to full spiritual maturity in Christ counts far more than the many that fail along the way in God's estimation. In the divine economy, one that is with God is worth immensely more than the many that are without him. The Heavenly Father only needs a willing vessel to pour his power into and work divine wonders. The faithful son that grows into spiritual maturity will be able to bear a son in his own stead. He that has grown to bear a son in the kingdom way will invariably be adopted by the Heavenly Father as a son in due time. He that has become adopted as a son by God has matured in Christ to become a member of the brotherhood of the christened in light and is much treasured by the universe.

The christened in light is deemed to be worthy of adoption on account of his willingness to be the sacrifice for others through love. It is on account of such nobility of spirit that he is chosen and called apart by God for full spiritual transformation in the Divine image. It is a call to go up the holy mount of transfiguration. Such is called to go up because God has found his heart to be acceptable for use to serve up Truth in love to others. The mountain of God teaches humility for no one can make it to the top by his own effort. He that aspires to scale to the summit must receive divine help. The climb to the summit requires total submission to the will of God for it is a quest that brings the seeker down on his hands and knees in total humility.

The christened in light are the chosen few out of the many called to serve God in exalted honor. They are the faithful few given to complete the journey started many years ago that many attempt but fail to complete. The christened in light is a rare seed that endures through the worst that the world dumps on him. He overcomes all that the prince of the darkness of this world throws at him because he is sheltered by the hand of God. Nothing can destroy such for God is with him so that his spirit remains indestructible. The christened in light may be pierced all over by the shrapnel and darts of foes that seek to destroy the innocent. His foes hate him because he lives to serve and offer up praise to God rather than to men. But because he lives to serve God with due honor, he is duly exalted in time to the chagrin and dismay of his enemies.

The faithful one that has been chosen to make it to the summit of God's mountain must return to his own as the elect of God. He must return to teach the new way of life in light for he has been bestowed with special insight into the heart and mind of the people. The heart of the people harbor their collective conscience and the mind of the people their collective consciousness. God's elect for the people can fathom their thoughts and their desires. He knows that it is not God's way when brother hates brother and when might claims to be right. He knows that the way that seems right to the faithless is the way of darkness that leads to death. It is a way that celebrates the coffin which is a dead-end. Rather the cross should be celebrated for it sets the bound spirit free into new life. The cross is the portal that lifts into the new life of regeneration but the coffin is the opening of the pit into the moribund.

The faithful that has been reborn into divine light through the cross must return and publish that which God has shown him. He that can now see and walk in the greater light must share what he has received with others that lack. He that has become a candle of God must hold up self so that others can see and know as well. The elect must be received for he brings a different light brighter and more searching than that which had been previously known. All who reject him reject the 'savior' that has been elected for the people. All who reject him risk losing everything for they will have no portion in the new life. All who receive him stand to gain Hope for they will begin a new life in regeneration. The elect one reborn in true light comes in peace with the spirit of the Divine in him to offer hope for those who desire to know. He will be the cause for jubilation for those that yield to embrace Truth. Those that are given to embrace must be the candle stick to hold him up so that others too may see and know as they have.

The christened in light are connected in a universal web of

truth, light, love and life that reflects the divine mind. Even though it may not seem like it to the casual observer, it is this mind that is managing the present age to its pre-destined end so that a new and better can begin. When the new age unfolds, the golden spirit of universal brotherhood will be the order of the day. The reborn in divine light will inherit the old and usher in the new for they are the eagle spirits that gather where the carcass of the old is. They are the rare precious seeds carefully chosen from the old that will be the seedlings for the new.

The mind of God can be fathomed from the words of Holy Scripture. Those words form impressions and constitute pictures that can be seen with the eye of the spirit. The pictures are not obvious for there are wisely disguised by both time and Divine will. The disguise of time will not allow certain pictures to be perceived until the due season divinely appointed for their knowledge comes about. Even in the season appointed for due knowledge, the things that constitute hidden wisdom are revealed only to the noble in spirit so that they may never be profaned by the unworthy. God is not secretive for all things are there to be seen and known. But yet many things remain hidden in open view so that only those that seek in truth and love may find them. The dimmer the light is the poorer that mankind's vision is but the greater the light is the clearer things become. The absence and paucity of love in the heart limits understanding but where love abounds wisdom shows forth in daily living.

When studied in the purest of light, the words of scripture show orderliness, harmony and the certainty of God's purpose. It shows the purpose of the Creator that pulses with concerned love for his creation. As the faithful believer matures in faith to step into purer and greater light, it becomes as though he can see further and search deeper. It is at this time in his life that he begins to see all things clearly. It is then that the words of scriptures come together in harmony to present a picture that makes plain all things about God, man and the relationship between them. From thereon he that walks in that purer and greater light will no longer be deceived for the veil of enlightenment has been lifted for him.

The faithful one that walks in the greater light will know as he is prepared to know. The more that he is prepared to receive will be the more that he finds when he seeks. Victory loves preparation and always favors those who are ready to receive. For the faithful believer that walks in the greater light it becomes as if he has received a new device that contains everything that man knows, will ever know and needs to know. The Father, Son and Spirit find agreement in the one that walks in greater light to make all things possible for him. Such a one has intermeddled with all-wisdom. It is as if he has received a wonderful device to enable him realize the amazing and glorious. He must dedicate his life to learn to master that device for it makes a host of services available to its custodian. It provides man with all the tools that he will ever need and makes an infinite array of services available at his fingertips. The custodian of that box who masters its use will be a god among men for it contains the impressions of the mind of God which is the consciousness that courses through the universe.

The present age is drawing ever closer to its demise. Even as it gasps for its last breath, the last remaining pictures that point to mankind's future are coming into clearer focus. Humanity has entered into Daniel's lot and finds itself in pre-judgment. All who have been chosen will have the key of understanding given to them. All who are rejected will be left to keep stumbling in darkness and follow the blind masses on to the very end. The greater light of the Divine is slowly but surely spreading. At the apex, it will be as if the sun has risen to set no more and day has banished night forever. Sadly many are poised to miss out on this due to unbelief and faithlessness but to God's glory others have come into its knowledge as due.

Chapter Notes

- ✓ The good fight won and race finished in victory is to pass the baton of the noble to a worthy receiver.
- ✓ The worthy son is the worthy fruit produced from a good tree that is so affirmed before God.
- ✓ The heart of the cross is the portal into the congregation of just men that is the living church.
- ✓ The faithful are chosen to be bestowed with special insight into the heart and mind of the people.
- ✓ The sons always bring a light brighter and more searching than that previously known.
- ✓ The pictures within scripture are disguised both by time and divine will for only true seekers to find.
- ✓ Those things that are known in the greater and purer light constitute hidden wisdom.
- ✓ The faithful that steps into the purity of the greater light can see further and search deeper.
- ✓ Divine light affords many tools and makes an infinite array of services available to the faithful.

Love's cord that binds all faithful hearts

Is the concord of praise of joyful tongues

For all in creation that reflect God's glory

Find harmony through acknowledging him

Chapter 13

THE EMBLEM OF HOPE

The believer that diligently feeds on the word of Truth and partakes worthily of grace through Christ will have his old self surely and steadily die. A new man will come alive within him remade in light through redeeming love and divine transformative power. The man of the old nature is earthy and weighty. His destiny is death but the man of the new nature is starry and light. His destiny on the other hand is life in eternity. He that has become transformed in his inner man to become the starry and light has become spiritually buoyant. No longer will he be bound to the earthy for he has overcome the world to find a place among the exalted. Such is one who will prevail over whatever challenges that he encounters in life through faith in God. In effect, the spirit within him has become fitted to pass through anything that stands in his way for he has become a man for all seasons and ages that cares more for the heavenly but less for earthly things.

Man's life on earth can be likened to a ship sailing on the

high seas. There are many who are not able to navigate through the stormy seas of life. Such are like ship-wrecked mariners overcome on life's stormy seas. Their ships are wrecked for lack of proper piloting and a reliable guidance system to warn them of perilous weather ahead. Life is a blind foray into uncharted waters for the ill-informed and oblivious. Such live as fodder for the predatory masterminds of the world who thrive on men's misadventures and misfortunes. Having lived without light for a long time, the spiritually blind do not know better and have become slaves to the prince of this darkness of the world. Most that are spiritually enslaved are creatures of the flesh that love the world too much and have lost their souls therein.

He that loves the ways of the world will hate the ways of God for both are diametrically opposed. The inevitable result of choosing the way of the world is spiritual death that renders mankind's earthly sojourn meaningless in the end. However there are a few able to sail through the world guided by the monitoring system of the divine eye positioned high above. This monitoring and guidance system is the all-seeing and knowing Heavenly Father who dutifully watches over his children on earth. These well-guided ones do not live as most others that are blind do. Rather they take their cue on daily living from the 'eye' above. He that is being guided by the Divine has committed to put his trust in God and serve him. Such a believer no longer labors in his own flesh and for his own gain but is led in spirit to serve God's purpose in all that he does. For such the unseen hand of God will always be near to protect, direct his footsteps and endue him with pertinent knowledge.

He that has the hand of God near to direct his life is distinct in his ways for he has been separated from blind humanity. There is a marked glow that shows from within him for his heart has become an altar lit with the flame of love. This glow is the emblem of hope and comes about as the faithful believer gets closer to the heart of God in spirit. It is the mark of the spirit that has been purified in truth and justified before God. Such a believer has the wellspring of life in him for his mouth will speak forth healing truth abundantly to those willing to embrace. He speaks Truth that is spiritually distinctive from verses of scripture memorized and quoted vainly for self-glory. But the words of Truth that he speaks forth are filled with the essence that breaks stony hearts, encourage faltering steps, feed hungry souls and lift lowly spirits.

Divine wisdom spills forth from him who walks in the light of greater understanding for he has stepped out from the shadowy into full light. Such is one who no longer sees in part but with full clarity and focus. Therefore he will begin to find good and better things with each passing day. There is no end to his amazement for he is given to travel on life's parkway where contentment is found. He will begin to care less for the things of the world as he realizes that his needs are divinely provided for and his wants easily met. Because he finds contentment in that which God provides, he becomes immune to the wear and tear of the world. As a result of that, time appears to slow down for him and age crowns him with graceful wisdom.

The wisdom from above is dispensed on a need to know basis. It is dispensed when the believer has been duly prepared and ready to receive it. Spiritual growth and readiness are realized by diligent study and obedience to the words of Truth. The more that mankind learns about and lives in faithful obedience to the word of Truth, the more the Heavenly Father reveals himself to the seeker. More of the divine nature is revealed when mankind desires and hungers for knowledge on how to come into fellowship with God. Divine wisdom is not dispensed because the believer wants to know but because he needs to know. Each golden nugget of wisdom is given when the due season for that knowledge to be known comes about. Although the Heavenly Father knows all things, he only reveals the needful things to the believer. It is like manna which must be received and eaten fresh each day. God does not haste because he is never late and he does not waste because he always has a good measure of all things. Rather he follows an orderly pattern that is borne of long suffering patience and good hope.

He that has grown to intermeddle with divine wisdom will begin to understand the universal language of all creation.

It is by divine wisdom that the key of understanding to unlock and give insight into all things is received. With such a key the ear of the spirit will begin to hear what everything around is communicating. It is language expressed inaudibly that can be clearly perceived. Although inaudible, it makes mental impressions on the mind when the believer is tuned in spirit to hear it. He that has been bestowed with this key must take the high road in all things in life. The world does not take kindly to such and so he must always seek guidance from above so that he can remain anchored in peace to have his endeavors remain pleasing to God. He must remain focused on the high things that are pleasing to God so that the antenna of the spirit within him can remain in tune with the Divine impulse. On a cautionary note, when the antenna of the spirit wanders and shifts away from the lofty, then the mind inevitably becomes flooded with the distracting stream of the mundane.

He that has received the key of knowledge must guard that which he has received with due care. His lifestyle must change to that of the 'gardener' into whose care are entrusted the precious seeds that are self-contained with the amazing. He must have the patient wisdom to cultivate and bring out the rare things which have been preserved in those seeds by the Divine. He must master the call that makes life to rise up from sleep and the entombed to spring forth in freedom's dance. He is one called to become the diligent gardener fit to tend Eden's garden.

Therefore he must commune daily through meditation and prayers with the Heavenly Father whom he must live to please. He must care little for the praise of men but look to serve God and humanity sincerely in humility of spirit so that his offerings of love may be well received above. If he is faithful in doing so, the Holy Ghost will inform him about the right seeds to plant and the Holy Spirit will enable him to tend the plants. He will be given to walk along calmly in the knowledge that God will be with him in life always.

There is a certain harmony and orderliness that surrounds life when mankind's footsteps are divinely guided to walk on the righteous path. Such a guided life will be fully settled in Christ to dwell in spiritual fellowship with other members of the divine household. Such a guided one does not walk alone but walks in the company of countless messengers for he has joined the fellowship of the justified that gather around the mercy seat of God. The latter are such that are able to eat of the fig of the tree of life. The fruit of the fig tree is not like that other kind which looks good to the eye but turns out to be bad for man's spirit. The matriarch Eve chose with her eyes instead of her faith and unleashed darkness on mankind. The fig tree bears the fruit of wisdom in accordance with man's obedience and faithfulness in the heavenly way. It is for the pure of heart. The fig tree bears that which the noble in spirit wish from it in faith. It is a wishing tree that accommodates the seed-thoughts of those who have passed judgment before God. Many will try but only a chosen few will find the real tree for there is much wickedness hidden in men's hearts. He that seeks after the fruit of the fig tree must seek after the witness of God and not that of men. The spiritually blind judge by appearance but the pure of heart 'see' and know by faith. Mankind is easily fooled and the enemy does fool many but God cannot be fooled. The nuggets of wisdom are divine seeds entrusted to the faithful. Such are of precious value to humanity and serve to validate those chosen by God. Each one chosen in this light is a channel for divine wisdom and a spiritual giant who walks among men but communes with God in spirit. Such is perceived by those who have embraced Truth and value the real.

Truth washes the heart and imparts nobility to the spirit of man. The noble in spirit can see and know all things as due. If he knocks, the door is opened for him. If he seeks, he finds that which he seeks. If he asks, that which he asks for is given to him. Such that is noble in spirit is given to carry the passport of life for his soul has been reborn for eternal habitation with the Divine. He has become a son of God who together with the other sons traverses the heavenly stairway in twinkling light to bring knowledge from the starry realm down to earth. Such has joined the rank of the immortal beings that can impart life to the withered and dying things on earth. He that traverses the heavenly way in light is a petition bearer to God on behalf of other men. The Heavenly Father interacts with him and he in turn interacts with other men as a divinely appointed mediator. He is like a magnet charged with the essence of

Godliness. He must use that magnetic charge to draw men to God through truth, light and love on to eternal life.

The essence of the Divine is precious and need not be needlessly discharged. Such must be invested to lead blind men back into the light and love of God through Christ. The faithful must keep his flesh on a very short leash for it works to diffuse and discharge the divine essence. The believer that fails to put the essence of godliness to good use is of no use to God or the world for that matter. The salt must not lose its savor for such that does so will be no good for either the land or the dunghill. The faithful one must remain virtuous and firm in spirit so that he can stand on behalf of many that are not able to stand for themselves in the spiritual warfare that bedevils mankind. The chosen have been given access to that which will release many from the imprisonment of darkness and so must stand tall in this regard to be counted worthy.

He who has been charged with the divine essence must not rest on his laurels but must continue to grow in the fullness of the riches of God through Christ. The knowledge, wisdom, judgment and way of God are too deep for man to fully comprehend. The faithful must continue to knock, seek and ask so that he can remain continuously charged in fresh anointing. The power of the Divine is exhaustless and limitless. It can be applied in countless ways to achieve infinite results. It is by continuously reaching towards the Father that the chosen can keep discovering the new within the Divine and grow from glory to glory. Christ Jesus declared that the sons of God who follow after him will do greater things than he has done. In that regard, the chosen that is charged with divine essence has more areas in life to utilize and apply God's power today than his predecessors in days gone by.

The enemy often lulls the unwary into a state of arrested spiritual development. The latter is a kind of spiritual dwarfism where the believer that could have been a giant in God's kingdom falls way short of his potential. He that could have been a Colossian remains a Galatian. He could never defeat the beast of his flesh in 'Ephesus' or move the boulder of material lust out of the way in 'Philippi'. The enemy reasons that if he cannot stop the spread of the kingdom of God that he can at least retard its progress by enticing mankind into sin through the lust of the flesh and earthly material. It is a very effective ploy for the laborer for God is often weary and running on empty. Therefore many professed laborers for God come to compromise their faith walk and settle for much less on account of weariness along the way. The sojourner on the path of righteousness takes a lot of battering from a spiteful world. But it is in the state of weakness that the power of God is made manifest to buttress the faithful. It is also in this state of weakness that the believer will stumble if he does not remain vigilant in spirit.

The key to victory over the beast of the flesh is to remain

covered spiritually and never take off the full armor of God. The key to victory over the boulder of material lust is to continue in sacrificial charity. The faithful believer must never be found spiritually naked nor fail to do what he can for the needy. Hoarding will turn off the faucet of grace and scuttle the vessel of hope. Failure in these areas leads to the idling of the spirit. The idle spirit is the playground of the prince of darkness. The believer will be flooded with the stream of the mundane in his mind when he is idling in spirit. There is never a good time to let one's guard down in the kingdom way for the enemy never quits. To remain victorious in the way, the faithful must keep away from that which he has been forewarned about. The things that he has received forewarning about are those which will spiritually discharge him that aspires for righteousness. The anointing is precious but it must be used for the enlightenment of humanity through Christ. The faithful must obey as God commands for it is by so doing that he will be endued with knowledge to keep him prepared to battle victoriously for God.

Chapter Notes

- ✓ Transformative power is availed to remake the believer that partakes worthily of grace.
- ✓ The faithless that live without light for a long time become slaves to the prince of darkness.
- ✓ The faithful that puts his trust in God will have his steps directed to live under divine protection.
- ✓ There is a glow that shows from within the heart that has become an altar lit with the flame of love.
- ✓ Divine wisdom is dispensed on a need-to-know basis and availed to the believer ready to receive.
- ✓ The believer bestowed with the key of knowledge must cultivate the rare and precious with patience.
- ✓ Truth washes and imparts nobility to the faithful to make his spirit able to know in true light.
- ✓ The power of the Divine is exhaustless and can be applied in infinite ways to do the amazing.
- ✓ The believer in arrested spiritual development idles in spirit and is soon flooded with the mundane.

A grander tapestry of life will be unveiled

As all the parts take their rightful places

Then will majesty of Creator and creation

Be displayed to be seen by all in true light

Chapter 14

THE REVITALIZED LIFE

The spirit is purified and wiling to serve God long before the flesh becomes conditioned to do so. There is a reconfiguring of the body that begins to take place as the faithful commits his heart totally to serve God. The believer that commits to God will begin to get rid of so many things of his old nature. He is in effect shedding the 'weight' of the world. He is being streamlined in mind, body and spirit so that he can be more effective in his fellowship with the Divine. He will also realize that he is being much more productive in his daily living for he will be doing more with less than he could ever do in the past.

He has begun to experience the redeeming power of Divine love to add value in things, people and situations by making them better. It is through the power of redemption that God validates those things, people and situations falsely judged, rejected and deemed unworthy by the world. It is the means by which God validates those things deemed to be of marginal or no value by the spiritually blind. It is by the process of redemption or making the earthly useful for heavenly purposes that the believer finds new life through the light and love of Christ.

The believer that is faithful in the way will come to dwell in the bowel of mercy of God soon enough. The bowel of mercy is a place of transformation where the spirit of the believer is reborn and his body redeemed in light. It is in the bowel of mercy that the faithful is grafted on to the tree of life. It is a cocoon for the preparation and readying before the sons of light are 'unveiled' to be perceived by those who seek after Truth. The son must first know who he is in spirit and live accordingly long before others come to know. The bowel of mercy is a place of spiritual retreat from the worldly where one is in the world but not of it. It is a place of consecration where the human and divine become merged for a common purpose. It is also a kind of infirmary where the 'sickly' old-self is reborn into the 'revitalized' new in Christ.

God knows that the faithful in the bowel of mercy is helpless in dealing with certain worldly concerns and issues. He knows that there are things that demand his attention that he is unable to take care of in that season. Therefore the divine spirit intercedes for him in those matters to meet those needs. The Spirit of God orchestrates all things to work together for good in the life of the faithful that dwells in the bowel of mercy. All things pertaining to faith, family, business and the future will be divinely orchestrated to come out right for him in the long run. However life in the bowel of mercy demands much patience. Therefore such that are in the bowel of mercy must learn to tarry and wait for those moments when space, time and divine purpose converge to effect the miraculous for him. He must learn to hold the wings of faith stretched out so he can be lifted up when the divine wind rises. He that dwells in the bowel of mercy has been called to give all to God. In return, the Heavenly Father will make adequate provision for him in the necessities of life. The dweller in the bowel of mercy has entered into a bond from which he can never be separated. It is to such that God has promised never to leave or forsake.

The faithful that dwells in spirit under mercy has a sense of peace that pervades his life. It is a form of peace that prolongs life and affords the believer many years of victorious living in Christ. Age seems to melt away to be replaced by a youthful and vigorous outtake on life. It is then that the believer comes to know the peace that passes all understanding. His fear and worries will be replaced by a spirit of power that is very comforting for he has been become joined to the Divine.

Peace within comes when mankind becomes joined in spirit with the Divine. Such that is so joined must begin to think lovely thoughts and to intercede in prayer for others for God will readily accommodate his requests. The spirit holds sway in life to govern all endeavors for the believer that dwells in the bowel of mercy. The flesh may tend to rear its' ugly head intermittently to take command of life but the dweller under mercy is given to overcome such distractions by asking for divine help through prayers. It takes some time and much struggling for the spirit to wrestle total control away from the flesh. He who has been able to do so must keep the flesh bound so that he may have glorious victory in all areas of life. It takes some time to learn this Truth. He that learns it has found the key to reaping the full benefits of the new life through Christ.

The faithful believer who dwells in the bowel of mercy has been grafted into the tree of life. He is one that has become righteous before God so that his name is written in the book of life. Therefore he must walk on the righteous path in all his endeavors. He may walk alone there for a season but it is the way that leads to eternal life. He must not follow the crowd for such choose to travel on the road of worldliness fraught with danger on which many perish. The road ordered for the righteous may be long, winding and wearying. But it teaches patience and affords the experience that sustains faith.

The path ordained for the righteous is transformation way on which the true self is found. The believer that travels on it will get home safely where much rejoicing awaits him. He will join the everlasting song of the victorious in faith. The essence of the everlasting is yielded in the agonizing crucible endured on the long and winding way of Christ.

The temporary discomforts of the way fuel the fire that purifies the soul. All who are tried and proven in this fire will forever march in God's army in collective order with other saintly souls who live to serve the divine will.

He that dwells in the bowel of mercy must learn to keep himself as a vessel ready for service and to tarry for God's call. The ear of his spirit must always be tuned and his eyes focused on the heavenly. The world may not yet know that he is a chosen vessel but that should never hinder his vision or mission. He knows who he is in the divine fold and that is what matters most. This knowledge should sustain and keep him till the time appointed for his unveiling for all to know. He is in God's select program and has to have trust fully that he who has brought him this far will finish what has been started. Therefore he must remain worry free and have his focus always on how to change the earthly for better in the light of Christ.

God knows about the 'infirmity' or worldly needs of the faithful one under mercy. As previously mentioned the Heavenly Father will always accommodate his petitions and requests in good faith. This is the key that avails much for him who dwells under mercy. It is for this reason that such must never cease from asking through prayers. It is the key that unlocks the heavenly vault for him. Prayer constitutes the voice recognition system that activates the door. Heaven hears all under mercy for their voices have been divinely programmed for access into Providence.

He who has been programmed can move mountains, break stones and shape metals with his 'voice' for he has power that speaks into the core of all things. The intentions of his heart and his actions must always be for the welfare of humanity so divine light can shine for all. The endeavors of all such under mercy should be for the uplifting of mankind. When that is the case, goodness will prevail, men will give God due praise and the wicked may reconsider their ways. He that lives 'mercifully' in this way has become the divine instrument for mankind's new glorious awakening.

There are times of spiritual lull in the life of the believer. This is natural and due to the bio-rhythm or ebb and flow of the flesh nature. For this reason, the faithful must always set aside time daily for praying and studying the word of Truth. At least, the wake up times of the morning and the bed times of the evening must be set aside for this purpose. He who is dedicated in this way and remains faithful to Truth written over the tablet of his heart will always receive from that which mercy avails. He will never be found naked but will always be fitly clothed spiritually. Above all, he will always remain anchored in peace even though he may be surrounded by the storms of life.

There is a time appointed for all borne of the bowel of mercy to reach a critical mass. This is the time of the great unveiling that everything in creation waits for. It can be likened to the blooming of wild flowers over a field in

Spring time. The latter do not sprout or appear individually but in mass on heaven's cue. All things in creation share a universal precept. It is an awareness that dates back to the foundation of time. Everything in creation is 'encoded' to know that a time will come when all the parts in God's creation will know their true functions and roles. As the parts know themselves and assume their true roles, the whole will become better known. Only then will the grandeur and majesty of creation together with the goodness of the Creator be fully understood.

Mankind has only been scratching the surface as he seeks for a way to fully open God's gift package to humanity. When the time of full understanding comes, all who have remained certain and strong of faith will know in fullness in the great dawn. Then it will become clear to all that a new regime of the spirit has taken over the world for mankind will be induced by brotherly love and entrained in an uplifting draft that no one can resist.

All who dwell under divine mercy are the vanguard of humanity's great dawn. They wield the sword of the spirit for their power is in their words. They speak to break the resistance of the stony hearted and cause the disobedient to yield. They speak in humility to serve and not for self-glory. They speak to share and to help fulfill the Truth. They love Truth and the way of Christ. Their life's calling is to share the knowledge and light of God in love above everything else. They do not live to impress men but to faithfully testify about God's goodness to mankind wherever and whenever there is an attentive ear.

Some may wish them to be silent but they cannot be muted for it is the Spirit of God that wills and acts through them to speak forth. It is the spirit that endues them with knowledge about what the issues to speak to. It is all divinely purposed to show that God is alive and dwells in them. They carry the burden of the word of Truth to the unbelieving masses as living witnesses to the veracity of God's promises and the reality of his existence. Many may reject Truth and their message of hope but the one soul who finds himself back into the divine fold is cause for much joy in Heaven and enough reason to justify their work on earth.

The spirit of God works through those who dwell under mercy to further the divine plan for mankind all over the world. Such that are under mercy share the mind of Christ and are therefore in spiritual harmony with the Creator. The spirit that is in harmony with the Divine is tuned to be in communication with creation. In effect, everything speaks to such for the spirit of the Creator that dwells therein is the same which courses through creation.

All things in creation come from one Divine source. For that reason, the faithful believer who is fully matured in spirit can communicate with all things in creation. He can understand the things that he has set his mind on for it is the spirit that communicates. The faithful believer that is connected in this way lives in the world in a way that all things in creation yearn for. It is the hope that all things in creation live in brotherly love as spawns of the same Heavenly Father. The one who does will have a foretaste of the glorious future appointed for humanity and live in that world now. He will be like a traveler in time that lives today in the spirit of the future that he has seen. While he patiently waits for the advent of that glorious future, he also makes sure to share the news about that which he has glimpsed and made possible through Christ with those who will pay attention. He who has glimpsed that future knows what to ask for from the Heavenly Father. Such that knows the right help to ask for is saved from expending precious time and energy on that which is not needed for the times ahead.

The faithful that dwells under God's mercy has been invited into the palace of the feast where his wishes are commands to the divine attendants. However he must cover himself in charity for it hides a multitude of sins and be merciful so as to remain blameless. His wishes must be for those things that lift up humanity for he has grown from faith into hope and now must grow from hope into charity. Since charity does not seek its' own or look for praise from men, his wants have to be simple for his life is now ordained to be used mightily by God. He is one that has come into the certain city on the certain day when the power of God is near to heal many. For that reason, the shopping list of his heart must contain only those things that bring honor and glory to the highest for as he thinks so do things turn out to be.

The Spirit of God searches for what is written in the heart of the faithful that dwells under mercy so as to make provision for those things. For that reason, the heart of such must dwell on the things that are true, honest, just, pure, lovely, virtuous, praise worthy and of a good report. To live under mercy translates into living charitably with all men. The wishes of the heart governed by charity are selfless and will meet the criteria listed. The right hand of the believer that lives charitably never withers for he will always receive from God. In effect, mankind's power to change his environment and influence people for better is amplified when mercy and charity abound. Wherever mercy and charity abound all earthly endeavors become dictated by the spirit of God and less by the flesh. Charitable living and selflessness rendered in purity of heart through Christ speaks to the power of sacrificial love and tells the story of redemption eloquently.

Chapter Notes

- ✓ The spirit is purified and willing to serve God long before the flesh becomes conditioned to do so.
- ✓ The bowel of mercy is a spiritual retreat where human and divine purposes become merged.
- ✓ The believer with peace within has the weariness of life replaced by a youthful and vigorous outtake.
- ✓ The road of the righteous is long and winding but it yields patience that makes for strong faith.
- ✓ The faithful are called to transform the earthly in accordance with the ideals of Christ.
- ✓ The wealth laid up for the faithful believer is that God will always answer his prayers.
- ✓ The grandeur and majesty of creation will be known when all parts know and play their roles.
- ✓ The matured in Christ is tuned to the Divine and can understand all things in creation.
- ✓ The faithful that stands under mercy feasts where his wishes are the commands of divine attendants.
- ✓ Redemption is effective in adding value to much through Christ for nothing is wasted in love.

Divine gifts are never glitzy or glossy

Not gilded to dazzle men's blind eyes

But poured into those strong of faith

And the firm in spirit fitted to receive

Chapter 15

ON THE ROAD OF HOPE

Faith has to be put to effective use in the work of God's kingdom on earth in order to meet the validation and the approval of Heaven. The desired and longed for hope of every faithful believer is to hear the Heavenly Father's welcoming approval. It should be the desire of every true believer to hear words of commendation from God when his earthly duty is done. The faithful believer that meets God's approval is a lighted candle given so that others may see and learn to follow the right way in life.

No son is worth his salt if he is not able to build on the foundation laid down by the father and build up the family business. The business for which the sons of God have been prepared and expected to fulfill is to reach those kindred spirits that have lost their way in the world. Those are the ones pre-destined for salvation that must be thrown the life line of redemption through grace. The redemption message framed in truth and love has to be shared so that the lost can find their way back into the

Divine fold. Only those already earmarked to do so can open their hearts to welcome Truth and unclench their fists to receive God's gift of love. But it takes the spirit of God speaking through his sons to induce those earmarked to act.

Those that have been earmarked for redemption will always feel out of place in this world. They may try as hard as they can but they will never be able to fit in this world for its ways are not in their nature. They will always feel as the proverbial square peg in a round hole. Life on earth will always be a case of wrong places and wrong times for them. The rewards and possessions of the world by which many validate themselves will neither bring them contentment nor peace. They will always feel empty and unfulfilled for they will feel like the fraud who is undeserving of that which he has. This is often the result when mankind chooses the way and spoils of worldliness instead of choosing God's way when his heart tells him to.

He that chooses the worldly has unwisely chosen to feed the bottomless pit of the flesh that can never be satisfied. Without intending to do so, he has become engaged in the winless battle of lust for material things that is a raging fire that can never be quenched. Deep down in the heart such will soon know that the way of the world cannot be right even though it is the path that many choose to follow. It is the recognition that the way of the world is not the right way that brings the seeker to the crossroad of life. It is when he has come to this crossroad of life that mankind can decide either to continue on the road of 'hope-lost' or change course to the road of 'hope-resurrected'.

Most men choose to seek safety in the company of others. They will continue to trudge along the road of 'hope-lost' with the rest of mankind unless there is divine intervention in their lives. But a few willing to listen to their hearts will get off that road and get on the road of 'hope-resurrected'. It is only when man is willing to make this switch regardless of the immediate cost that he can truly open his heart to God. Only then can he unclench his fists to receive the nurturing bread of life that will change and recharge his life with a heavenly-ordained purpose. Mankind must be willing to look away from the world so that he can 'see' and find his destiny with God. He must be willing to travel alone if need be but during that time all that ails him will begin to flee. He will begin to find answers to the issues of life that bedevil him. He will overcome his feelings of dejection and come into blissful resurrection of spirit. He will come into increasing peace for he will come to realize that far from being alone the Heavenly Father watches over him indeed.

God will usually send help to that one that stands at the crossroad of life to guide him over to resurrection road. There will always be an occasion that tips the scale for the sincere seeker and encourages him to find his destiny with God. Help will come to encourage and guide him in the way lest he becomes totally discouraged. Life for the beginner that seeks after Christ can be very bewildering and disconcerting. It takes some time to change gears and understand that the mode of travelling on God's path is different from the mad dash of the world. On the righteous path, one yields his will and is conveyed along in the spirit of God along a pre-destined route.

The footsteps of the faithful believer are directed along a path divinely chosen for him. It is a road for the patient traveler that may prove to be long and constraining but it will get him 'home' to the Father above with little wear and tear. However, it is not so with the way of the world. There the unbeliever dashes about in his own understanding as he takes unnecessary risks and shoots randomly as if in a seemingly dark alley where he often misses more than he hits the target. Such is like one that aims for an elusive target that always moves and mocks him to try harder. Furthermore, at the end of it all he often finds to his disappointment and chagrin that the prize promised is never that delivered after all his troubles.

The young believer that aspires for life on the path of the righteous must learn its patient ways. He must have someone to watch and learn from who has gone much farther along or that has come to maturity in the way. It is in this arena of breast feeding the up-and-coming that mastery in the work of faith and God's commendation is received. The matured in Christ must put his faith to effectual use by nurturing the young in the way in love. The matured believer with experience in the way must share the light, point out pitfalls to avoid and encourage the young up-and-comer in faith to be patient. The elder must teach and expound the word of God to the young in faith. He must teach him about the uplifting power of the psalms and spiritual songs. He must demonstrate the way of sacrifice that sustains faith and brands the faithful as God's own. He must be the medium by which the young come to experience Divine grace through Christ. This is very necessary in the early and formative days of faith for it enables the young in the way to find spiritual focus and not be easily distracted to be led away.

The spiritual eye of the young must be opened to the limitless possibilities and richness of the gifts that he can obtain along the road of hope. He has to be taught so that his heart can focus on the high and lofty things that will yield the good things in life for him. It is like the new born infant that is aware that a new world surrounds him. But everything still remains a blur for he is not yet able to focus on an object. In order to help him gain focus, an object must be held fixed in front of the infant before he can reach out and touch it.

The young believer may have his heart and intentions in the right place but without someone to guide him he will not be able to produce the desired results. The eagle must teach the scion how to put away his fears and exercise the muscles of his wing so he can fly. He must do so in order that he may soar to the exalted realm that holds out warm and ready hands to avail him great vision. Without spiritual vision nothing of significance can be experienced and obtained from God. In the absence of spiritual vision, mankind stumbles around mostly in the darkness of worldliness and slip-slides in earthiness.

Divine gifts and riches are not glossy on the outside or gilded to dazzle the eyes of mankind. Rather there are bestowed and poured into the faithful believer that is spiritually prepared and ready to receive them. Such gifts can only be perceived by the beholder whose spiritual eye has been opened. The gifts of God can only be perceived and received in mercy by the erstwhile blind that has been made to see. He that can see can be shown the right road to follow. Once he has started on that road, he may appear to be alone but he will not be for he will be travelling in the company of an unseen host. Though he may seemingly walk alone for a season, yet he will be guided and conveyed along in the spiritual stream of upward bound souls where God's power is manifested.

The spiritual dynamic that makes the power of God to abound operates on two important principles. Firstly, it must be used for making humanity better. Any step that leads away from darkness towards light through love helps to make humanity better. The gift from God is a gift for all. Secondly, the more that a divine gift is used in serving God leads to a greater outpouring of divine anointing and power. On those two principles rest the grounding of grace, the premise of goodness and the promise of mercy. To live for all and not for self is what defines divinity. To live for self and not for others is the reason for damnation of mankind's soul. Damnation is the result when God turns a deaf ear to mankind's prayers. It deserves to be emphasized that the promise of resurrection is not realized except through charity, prayer and thanksgiving.

The Heavenly Father readily gives in wisdom to the noble-hearted soul who receives and shares spiritual gifts for the benefit of the people. To do otherwise is to profane the gift and mock the giver. Let the profane man beware that God is not mocked and nothing gets by him. The divine gift that is profaned, used crudely and not put to its destined purpose will fill the atmosphere with smoke. Smoke is cloud that bears no rain water but irritates men's eyes and hampers vision. The gift received with thankfulness and tendered to the people produces a brilliant smoke-free light that allow men to see clearly so as to choose the better in life. Such is light availed only to the honorable in the sight of God. It is light that can never be put out by the evil wind of darkness. Such light affords wisdom that will always glow with an incandescent purity.

The wisdom of the world presumes to cloak itself in age and experience. Such wisdom is often borne of the earthly and serpentine. This can present a stumbling block for the ignorant that is not able to perceive in spirit. The wisdom from above is not cloaked in age or experience. It is a gift bestowed on the pure of heart and noble in spirit by the Heavenly Father. It is 'Eli' perfected in 'Samuel' and 'Paul' perfected in 'Timothy'. It is the son awakened in the true likeness of his father. The son is the perfection realized during the journey on the upward bound way so that life may reign supreme. The Father is the lifelong labor made in self-sacrifice to keep the trail of perfection open so that Hope may always abound.

The gift to the self is imperfect as it seeks to glorify the imperfect self. The gift from the pure of heart to another that is without vaunting or flaunting is perfect. Such is always commended by the Heavenly Father. That which is commended by the Divine has great intrinsic value locked within where neither thieves nor robbers can break in. The way to unlock that bestowed within is through humility and sincerity for it is borne of love tendered in mercy. He that gives out of a pure heart is the noble soul that will be given to soar higher in spirit, shine brighter before mankind, travel much farther on the wings of time, and do greater things in life.

Chapter Notes

- ✓ It takes redeeming love to open hearts to welcome Truth and receive divine gifts.
- ✓ The misguided that lusts after worldly spoils has chosen to feed the bottomless pit of the flesh.
- ✓ The road of Hope may be long and constraining but it leads home with little wear and tear.
- ✓ The true believer must demonstrate the way of sacrifice and denial that brands faithfulness.
- ✓ New life begins when the eye is opened to the limitless possibilities and gifts availed thru Hope.
- ✓ The divine gifts are not glossy or gilded to dazzle the eyes but bestowed within the believer.
- ✓ Divinity embraces the faithful that lives for all and not self but damnation of soul shadows the selfish.
- ✓ The wisdom from above is the gift of truth, age and experience blended in a cocktail of life.
- ✓ Divine gifts have great intrinsic value locked in where neither thieves nor robbers can break in.
- ✓ God casts his reflection on the faithful so that by them others can cease from stumbling in darkness.

Peace comes from not having fear of death

When the old within has made place for a new

Then the enduring and ever-lasting are received

With certainty of faith and in freedom of love

Chapter 16

FROM SEED TO TREE

The aspiring believer can only be transformed into the similitude of Christ if he is willing to pass through the heart of the cross. To pass through the heart of the cross is a Divine calling that only God the Father asks of the chosen. The heart of the cross represents the crossover point between the temporal and the eternal. The believer that willingly endures the attendant suffering to pass through the heart of the cross is given to commute between the exalted realm and the earthly plane. Only the faithful that can soar to the exalted heights in spirit can be of glorious service to God on earth.

The heart of the cross is the point of separation where the world has cast off the believer so to say. By the same token, it is where the believer makes the commitment to double down on God no matter what. The heart of the cross is where the faithful is abandoned by friends, family and many on account of his uncompromising love for God. It is a place where the faithful is grossly and unfairly misunderstood, mischaracterized, derided and often mocked. The heart of the cross is the crucible where the crucial choice between immortality and mortality is made. It is the portal through which the faithful enters into the realm of the perfecting of men into the divine image as sons of God on earth.

The faithful that has passed through the heart of the cross has joined the congregation of the mighty in spirit that stand before God. Such are the sons that walk in greater divine light to oppose spiritual wickedness and afford justice on earth in God's name. At the heart of the cross and beyond is where the spirit has overcome the flesh. It is where the offending portion of the old self is entombed and from where the matured in Christ steps forth to serve God faithfully. It is at that point that the spirit becomes ascendant to lead the flesh always.

The faithful one who passes through the heart of the cross becomes a son of the covenant adopted into the household of the Heavenly Father. He will no longer belong in one place but will belong everywhere. He will no longer belong with anyone but will belong with all men. Such is one who belongs to all yet belongs to none. He will love all men but love God above all else. Such is divinely appointed to walk on earth without fear as God's proxy borne through love. The child of love thinks, speaks and acts in kind. He that has been borne through divine love has come into the place of regeneration where the old things can be made new again for love breeds life.

The journey to the place of regeneration is a long and wearying one that takes a great toll on the faithful. But it is a journey that leads to transformation in spirit, full maturity in Christ and eternity. He that seeks after it must be prepared to lose everything in the world in the interim before he can find that priceless gift in the end. He that finds it will gain everything back in the regeneration that follows in addition to eternal life with the Heavenly Father. It is a long and gradual process in which the tiny seed of faith planted in the believer's garden of the heart grows into full maturity as a tree of righteousness. Through this process the believer is washed in mind, transformed in spirit and fitted in body to serve God gloriously.

Regeneration is life triumphant that snatches victory from the jaws of death. He that has come into regeneration wills and acts under the divine impulse. The regenerated spirit sits at meat with Christ Jesus and the other sons of God under divine love. Such are availed knowledge and wisdom that affords mankind insight into the veiled. Victory in daily living comes about through insightful knowledge. Insightful knowledge is obtained through the Holy Ghost. It is knowledge that avails the words that make it possible to speak to the mountain that stands along life's path to move it out of the way. Problems appear in life but answers to them are found when God is near to empower the seeker with pertinent knowledge.

The faithful that has passed through the heart of the cross into regeneration will always have God near to help. He that is in the place where God is at hand is intimated with the information that he needs to achieve breakthroughs and attain victory in life.

Regeneration is the preserve of those who have passed through the heart of the cross and is the best reserved for last. The power that enables regeneration in the life of the believer comes only from the Heavenly Father who is the giver of life. It is power released exclusively in mercy from the Father to the chosen. He that has come into regeneration is able to receive directly from the throne of the Heavenly Father. He is a son who receives from the Father in mercy and is called to share with others in grace.

Regeneration opens up infinite possibilities and brings about amazing outcomes to the faithful. But much depends on the ability of each son to have his mind focused on the lofty and high things that are pleasing to God. The things that the heart dwells on are the things that mankind aspires to receive in life. The soul that is in regeneration is connected in spirit with the Divine Father and therefore able to bring about whatever the mind conceives through Christ. But he is also one who has been anointed in spirit to teach other men about the divine way. He must therefore remain a light that shines in the midst of darkness for that is his true calling above all else.

The faithful that has come into regeneration is a standard

of reference by which God measures his fellows. He will be constantly provoked in the world but such must learn to be forgiving and merciful always. Much has been divinely ordained for him to do with his time on earth for in regeneration either thoughts, words or actions can cause much to come about. Such is one who no longer gropes about blindly but is guided directly to the heart of every matter. He lives as a witness to men as one committed to truth, simplicity and orderliness in the service of God. He has no problems with telling Truth for it is often in trying to be everything to everyone that the infirm believer compromises faith. It is in trying to be liked by one and all that many seekers are never able to meet up with Christ.

It is in trying to win the praise of men that many believers drift away from the simple and orderly life into the complicated and entangling. The tangled web of life is the domain of the enemy of light who is the prince of the darkness of this world. The misguided, though well-meaning in intention, often falls into the trap of people pleasing to his painful regret. The tendency to please people above all is a slippery slope that often leads the unwary to make compromises and end up in unintended places. There is always a steep and costly price paid in compromising Truth either by trying to appease or keep up appearances with men. To deny or compromise Truth obscures light to invite darkness into mankind's heart. Truth is what defines God and is the foundation for the divine law. He that lives by Truth will have God ever near.

The believer that embraces Truth to live by it soon becomes a dwelling place of the Divine. Out of that heart will spring forth words that are filled with the power of God. Such a heart will become a wellspring of Truth and the transmitter of divine thoughts to mankind. Therefore such a heart that is purified in Truth must focus on uplifting thoughts for his mission in life is to model the way home to the Heavenly Father for others. He will duly become an earthly transmitting station that broadcasts Truth from above to all who hunger for righteousness and the true bread of life. He will come to know on earth as he is known in Heaven by God. In the same wise, he will come to know from Heaven as he is known on earth by men.

As the believer labors to share the message of Christ faithfully, the light of Truth will shine even brighter on, around and for him. His understanding of the veiled truths will deepen. The door of understanding will open widely for him so that his 'glimpse' of the Heavenly Father will become grander and fuller. The Truth that such is given to speak out become appropriate for every matter at hand as one fitly endued with divine wisdom. His words are far from frivolous but Truth directed at the heart of issues. Such are words that break the stony heart so that the goodness therein can be extracted to serve God. Such are also words that induce men of hard exteriors to yield so that they can be shaped into vessels of honor for God. The words of such a faithful heart purified in Truth make things happen for they contain seeds of the spirit of life that inject life into every situation addressed. Such a fountain of the words of life lives to ask, expect, and receive with thanks from God as well as to share with others in love. He is one well prepared to impregnate men's minds with the seeds of such good works that please the Heavenly Father. It is for this reason that he is called not to allow the seeds of his holy vessel to lie fallow but to spread them as needed and thereby plant a heavenly garden on earth.

He that is thusly engaged in cultivating the 'earthly garden that pleases God' is a favorite target of the enemy of light. The latter is always working against God's faithful ones to becloud the mind with earthly cares and worries. Cares and worries breed fear and doubt. Fear and doubt take the lens of the mind out of focus so that a spiritual shadow is cast over the life of the believer. Granted that God's faithful ones may seem to be in the midst of life's storms more often than not yet they pass through them into new and better places every time. When the believer is firmly anchored in faith by trusting God always, peace prevails within the heart even in the midst of life's storms so that he is protected and none the worse for wear.

The faithful one that has embraced Truth to live by it has divine immunity and is shielded from such troubles that will overcome others. He will be able to withstand the battering of life to carry on the good works by which the power of God is glorified among humanity. The most important work is the rescue of the souls lost in seemingly forgotten places that God deems worthy of redemption. The world may forget the erstwhile stranded and seemingly lost soul. But the Heavenly Father who never forgets makes provision for such who will yet prove to be worthy in due time through Christ.

Light catalyzes life but darkness retards it. In order for new life to emerge and flourish, light has to chase darkness away first. The message of Truth through Christ is the light that chases darkness away. The exalted into new life are separated from the world by Truth and the light of Christ. The separation can be likened to a membrane that has tiny holes that are smaller than the proverbial eye of a needle. In order to pass through the 'hole' to be exalted and commune in spirit with God, the faithful must become lowly in spirit through sincerity and humility. Communion with God is the heavenly side of earthly living. It is the small plot of land that costs dearly but wherein that very rare 'precious pearl of life' is hidden. The wise seeker is called to sell all he has if need be in order to afford that small plot. He that has passed through to the Heavenly side has exchanged the confining box of the earthly for the enduring and ever unfolding blossoms of the exalted Divine realm.

Chapter Notes

- ✓ The heart of the cross represents the crossover point between the temporal and the eternal.
- ✓ The heart of the cross is where the old is entombed so the new can step forth for glorious service.
- ✓ Spiritual transformation is realized when the tiny seed of faith grows into a tree of righteousness.
- ✓ The faithful that passes through the heart of the cross into regeneration will always have God near.
- ✓ The power of regeneration comes from God and is released in mercy from the Father to sons.
- ✓ The work done in regeneration is carried out through the spirit of God at all hours day and night.
- ✓ The purified heart is a depository from where words that are filled with spirit and power flow.
- ✓ The enemy uses fear and doubt to take the mind out of focus so as to mislead the infirm in spirit.
- ✓ The faithful sanctified in Truth has divine immunity from the things that will destroy other men.
- ✓ The light that the sons bring chases away darkness to catalyze the emergence and flourish of new life.
- ✓ Wisdom is to exchange the confining box of the earthly for the limitless blossoms of the heavenly.

The flame of wisdom is a rare gift that only glows

In minds rid of fear and doubt that love the truth

In feet guided to take timely and orderly steps

With open hearts that receive with due thanks

Chapter 17

UNDER DIVINE ILLUMINATION

The wiles and craftiness of the prince of the darkness of this world never ceases. Therefore the son of covenant must always seek greater understanding and knowledge in order to remain steps ahead. The people of God perish not for lack of good effort but mostly for lack of knowledge. Therefore the faithful believer must continuously seek to learn in the better light that comes from living obediently to God's laws. He must aspire for the knowledge and wisdom that is divinely imparted. He that abounds in such knowledge and wisdom will be protected from the evil intentions of the enemy. When greater understanding is followed with faithful living, a brighter divine illumination comes about in the life of the believer. He that is under that greater illumination will twinkle as a star of hope by which his fellows on earth may find their way. Such will ever twinkle as a star as long as he remains a source of enlightenment for other believers to follow after Christ. He will always draw from the well of divine wisdom and receive the wherewithal needed to help him be fruitful in all endeavors.

There are many believers who fall short and are not able to come into the place of greater light or divine illumination. They short-change themselves and fail to receive that which was theirs to possess. Such are the ones who got to the vestibule and walked away never to cross the threshold into the place appointed for them. They failed to step in by not searching out and meditating on the words of Truth. The faithful believer must have strong faith for only such are given strong vision. The seeker after Divine enlightenment has to enter alone into the place of light while there is room. He must not have fear for though he appears to be alone in his journey he is never alone but in the company of 'unseen' spiritual helpers.

As the faithful ponders on a matter of Truth, illumination comes into his mind in momentary flashes of divine inspiration. Veiled knowledge is progressively received from the Divine mind in trickle bits of information but the moment of full understanding is like the flash of lightening in its spontaneity. It is subtle and not as dramatic though. It only connects with the spirit that is ready and the mind that is prepared to receive. The flash of lightning illuminates the dark briefly but it is enough to reveal that which is concealed within. The brief revelation availed by lightning aids the seeker to maintain or change course as necessary. But it will not aid the guilty of heart for such are petrified by the thunder clap that soon follows suit.

The free in spirit is divinely appointed to harness the power of lightning to shred the wall of ignorance that encircles mankind. Lightning transports the ready mind from the present to make the future known. To harness the illumination of lightning is to ride the stream of light. The faithful believer given to ride the stream of light will master time and conquer space. He can travel to wherever needed to answer the Divine call and keep love's appointments. The latter is the mission of healing and restoration through Christ. Divine wisdom is obtained in glimpses in spoonful of love. It is timely distilled from the previously known and reveals itself in ghostlike streaks. It appears from beyond the wall which encircles human consciousness into the present. It is the transfusion of the divine ethos into the moribund in order to bring resuscitation and hope into it. It is the kiss of love that awakens the sleeper when God's day finally dawns for the believer. It is the comforting essence of the Holy Ghost.

The believer that is matured in Christ lives as the free in spirit under the mercy of God. The life fully lived in Christ is one where God's anointing flows freely from Heaven above to the believer below. The anointing works to lift up the less from his lowly state into a higher plane of spiritual enlightenment. It shines needed light so that the relatively blind can begin to see and walk in fellowship with God. It takes a heart willing to commit totally and sacrifice fully in love to help unbelievers embrace Truth. It takes the sort of love that will not let the redeemable go to waste. It is mentally and physically exhaustive work to help the unbeliever find the path of light through Christ. To break the stony heart or to soften the hardened mind is a noble endeavor but very hard to accomplish. It should never be for personal gain but should always be about one brother looking out for another's welfare. It is only when such is the case that the Spirit of God lends aid to make the work become fruitful.

It is only through selfless sacrifice and exemplary charity that faith abounds for the kingdom of God to be established. It is by selflessness and charitable living that the faithful grow into full spiritual maturity in Christ to become God's sons. The faithful have to be 'baptized' in the spirit of Christ in order to be like 'Christ'. Selfless sacrifice carried out in true charity is the baptismal font of Christ. To become Christ one must live like him. The mold has to be the same and the spiritual profile has to fit in the light of Truth and love. In the materially driven world of today, it has become increasingly difficult to live in selfless sacrifice. To be like Christ is a spiritual state that each seeker can realize if God has ordained such for him. It is only God that makes the seemingly impossible for many to become possible for some. The perfecting of the spirit sought after by many is availed by following in the footsteps and living in the way of Christ. It is the only way to be baptized in true light for it cannot be purchased or obtained otherwise. The faithful that has been 'baptized' in the spirit of Christ has met up with the Divine. His old self no longer exists for it has in effect been replaced with the essence of Christ. The new man within the believer that has met up with Christ is one matured in spirit and fitted for adoption as God's son. But he that aspires for such must first overcome the temptations of fame and fortune for that is the mountain in the way for many.

The aspiring seeker has to die in the old self through Christ so that a new can come to full life within him. He must be willing to live selflessly as well as sacrifice fame and fortune as necessary in order for that to come about. He that dies with Christ is given to rise with him also. Therefore the risen in Christ can give life to the dead in spirit. He can resuscitate the dead in sin to new life through Christ for the words of life spring forth from within him. Such is one who can sustain the living and restore the dying through his anointed words. He is able to reap life because he sows life. Life returns to him that passes it along to others. The universe makes room and affords a seat at the table everywhere for the sower of life for he lives as one with the Divine.

He that has died and risen with Christ seeks to have others hearts washed and purified in Truth so that they too can rise in the newness of Christ. This is his calling and nothing is of equal importance to him in life. Such is indeed a man of God but he may not look the part. He is not one the kind that looks saintly on the outside but is ugly within in the spirit as many who loudly profess to follow Christ turn out to be. Nevertheless, the risen in Christ is the saintly in spirit whose heart has been chosen by God as a dwelling place. When God dwells within the heart, the believer is led to devote his life to help the blind see, the lame walk and the dead in spirit live again through Christ. Spiritual blindness leads to a lack of defined purpose in life. Lameness leads to the inability to follow through and accomplish defined objectives. Whereas the dead in spirit can never experience the Divine for he lacks the means within to do so. He that has risen with Christ can help aspiring seekers find the missing that robs them of wholeness in life.

There is a season when the rains cease. This is when the window of grace is closed. This is the season of spiritual accountability when the Heavenly Father looks for figs from the tree that has blossomed with leaves. It is the season when God looks for evidence of Christ from those who profess to follow after him and have partaken of grace in his name. The evidence that God looks for is the heart that is baptized in Truth and lit with the flame of love for all. The close of grace is the season of reprimand for those who have partaken unworthily of grace. It is the season of reprimand for those who did not join the feast of charity in love but for personal gain. Such ones may have gained in the material but those things will come to be of little profit to them when it counts. Those that are reprimanded are not shakers but fakers of faith who look saintly on the outside but are ravenous wolves within.

The faithful that is free from reprimand is a true branch of the tree of righteousness that is laden with figs. The fig is the ability to understand the symbolic language that veils spiritual Truth. The fig is the key to understanding the mysteries of life and the kingdom of God. The platter of figs is about higher and purer Truth communicated with few words. It is the litmus test that ascertains faithfulness and maturity in the way. The fig is the same as the meat of Truth and requires the teeth of wisdom to chew down. Only those who have lived faithfully in the light of Truth to full spiritual maturity through love can understand the hidden things of the Divine.

He that bears figs can communicate with the Divine and all of God's own for the language is borne of same spirit. The fig is figurative language that is traceable to Heaven but applicable on earth. He that can eat figs can understand parables which constitute the language of calibrating earth with the standards of heaven. It is the language by which the Father communicates with his sons on earth. He who bears and eats figs has the attributes of godliness. Such is one who will be given to frame pictures with words with the effortless brilliance of undeniable Truth. A picture is the purest form of communication in that it speaks clearly without words so that there is no misunderstanding. The faithful eater of figs must share the offerings in love so that his fellows on earth may learn them. He that receives in mercy from the Heavenly Father is called to share with those who embrace Truth in good faith through grace. He that has mastered the way that leads to life must walk back to share with those who are yet to find same.

The faithful one that shares will have latter rain in life for God never withholds his tender mercies from such. The latter rain is the shower of blessing that leads into the refreshing and new. It is the dew of the latter rain given to sustain the fig tree. The essence of the fig is the nectar of the new wine which can only be contained by the new wine bottles. The latter are the faithful vessels molded in spirit after Christ who receive duly from God and share as love urges. Such vessels of mercy are the fulfillment of the Father's promise of love and the justification for wisdom. God makes provision for all the ingredients that the merciful needs so that the cocktail of his life is ideal as he serves humanity in love. It is the desire of God that the joy of the merciful be full for he is in covenant with the Divine as the representation of the passing of the former and beginning of the new in a foretaste of glory.

Chapter Notes

- ✓ The faithful under divine illumination is a star of Hope to help others find the true way.
- ✓ The faithful appear to walk alone but travel in the company of unseen spiritual helpers.
- ✓ Flashes of divine inspiration come to the faithful when the spirit is ready and the mind prepared.
- ✓ Wisdom is timely distilled from the known and revealed within the frame of the 'unknown'.
- ✓ God readily grants the petitions of the believer who has overcome temptations of fame and fortune.
- ✓ The faithful that sows in mercy reaps same for such returns to him that passes it along to others.
- ✓ The dead in spirit can never have experience of the Divine for he lacks the means to receive the pure.
- ✓ The advent season is when God looks for hearts purified in Truth and lit with the flame of love.
- ✓ Divine wisdom affords the key to understand the symbolic language that veils the everlasting.
- ✓ The essence of the tree of life is divine wisdom for those remade to be new wine bottles to receive.
- ✓ Mercy serves the golden rule well as fulfillment for love and justification for wisdom.

True fulfillment is found at meeting point

Where Heaven and earth embrace in love

For thereabouts in the sweetest concord

Wisdom whispers man's purpose to him

Chapter 18

CONTENTMENT WITH GODLINESS

The lack of thankfulness for the gifts received in grace through Christ is the chief reason that prevents many professed believers from coming into full knowledge of the Divine. Such are not able to find justification before God even though they have been led to the vestibule of Truth. He that is unthankful for what he has received in grace through Christ will become the malcontent in spirit. The unthankful is a hoarder that fails to share the things in his custody as ought with those that lack. Thankfulness to the Divine for life's gifts leads to contentment of soul. It leads to godliness and much gain but the malcontent in spirit will always have lack for he will never have experience of the Divine. Lack of contentment defines the selfish spirit that seeks after own gain. He that seeks his own gain under the cloak of serving God commits an egregious sin for he has deceived himself into mocking God.

Justification before God through Christ is realized by those who are pure of heart and noble in spirit. He that is noble in spirit is selfless and always thankful for life's gifts whether little or grand. The professed believer who partakes of grace by mixing the selfish ways of the world with the sacrificial ways of Christ chokes life out of the fellowship of love. He is an abuser and unworthy partaker of grace who will never grow to full spiritual maturity in Christ. He is keen to enjoy the rewards of grace but withholds his hand from sharing with others. He is a taker who seeks his own gain above Christ. He will never come to know and enjoy the true riches of God through Christ. Such may have earthly possessions but he will never have fulfillment. He is the fly in the ointment that ruins the anointing. Grace is shared within a communion of spirits bound together in the way of truth and love. The members bear each other's burden together in a commonwealth of spirits dedicated to love for all and service to God. Grace abounds within the commonwealth of Christ individually and collectively for the common good of humanity. The true way of Christ can only be walked and the blessings fully realized by the believer that seeks the welfare of all.

The unworthy partaker of grace lays an extraordinarily heavy burden on the worthy members of the fellowship of Christ by his misguided acts of selfishness. The worthy partaker is often burdened in spirit for he can perceive that there is a fly that ruins the feast of charity for all through selfishness and greed. It is like the rest of the body being affected when one part is infected. It makes the spiritual walk even more of an uphill task and leads to moments of spiritual discouragement for the worthy when he travels in company of the unworthy. But to God's glory grace suffices to sustain the worthy through all the troubles that visits him. Sadly the heart of the unworthy partaker of grace is in his left hand. He will never hear the still small voice of God for he does not walk on the righteous path. But the heart of the worthy partaker is in his right hand. Therefore he is always led along the path of righteousness to hear God's words of comfort. It is such comforting words of God's promise that reassure the worthy in grace that all will be well.

It is the comforting reassurance heard within the inner man that keeps the faithful believer laboring in worthy service for God. The worthy laborer knows that grace is divine provision that serves to nourish the soul so that the spirit within may abound fully in Christ. But the unworthy partaker who is not able to hear such comforting reassurance tends to misappropriate grace and is soon blinded in the way. He may abound in the material in the short term but he will never abound in areas that pertain to the Divine for he has set grace to naught. But the worthy partaker will abound in faith and grow in spirit to find the kingdom of God where he can have his heart's desires duly fulfilled.

Christ is the spiritual image and likeness of the Heavenly Father manifested in man. The faithful believer that has awakened in spirit in the full image of God through Christ will be duly satisfied in all his earthly desires. On account of unconditional love for God, he is often willing to suffer lack so that his spirit may abound in godliness in the fullness of time. It is such unconditional love that yields strong faith and total trust in God so that the believer can come to be duly adopted under divine mercy. The adopted is given to have ready access to the Divine heart so that he will not be denied anything that he desires. He may lose much along the way but he will gain back everything lost because goodness and mercy will follow him as one who is now at home with God in spirit.

All who are at home with God in spirit are connected with the Divine in a network of the exalted and noble of soul. There is a spiritual hierarchy that governs this network where God can be likened to a super computer, the sons to servers and aspiring believers as personal computers. The sons are connected to each other and to the heavenly Father in a universal web of life and love of goodness. Each aspiring believer that seeks in good faith can in due season be changed from a personal into a server computer or saved in accordance with divine will. However many of the personal computers are infected by the virus of the world and precluded from this 'transformation' or salvation. There is too much of the world in their memory banks. The information that they receive from the servers is often corrupted by worldliness that lurks in their hearts. The aspiring believer that desires to serve God with glory must shield himself from the worldly and keep the vessel of his life free from the corruption of worldliness for that is his reasonable service to God.

Sadly many believers let their guards down and are not able to remain shielded from the corruption of the world. Therefore only a select number of the personal computers are able to undergo the change to become servers. Only a chosen number of believers will be ordained to have the tent of their tabernacles enlarged to become true shepherds to guide others in the way of light. Only those who have kept up the fire walls through faith to protect themselves from the corrupting and infectious in the world are chosen. These are the few who keep faith with God always to become sanctified in Truth. They walk along the strait and narrow path. They refuse to nibble on the cookies that poison the mind left behind by the bewitching and predatory agents of darkness that loiter in the dark alleys of the world. These few have not cluttered the memory banks of their minds with the worldly and so have left ample room for the spiritual to abound therein.

The mind of the 'super computer' Father is always in communication with the 'server computer' sons. The communication between the Father and his sons is in source code of divine Truth. It is written in the binary language of Truth which in effect is a language of this or that, yes or no and dos and don'ts. This is the meat of the word of God hidden from most believers but there to be searched out by the faithful and noble in spirit as due. The

Father is the source of this information and communicates them to the sons as needed in real time. The Father speaks in a universal language heard with the ear of the heart and understood within the spirit as the meat of the word. It is language for the 'certain and firm in spirit' who walk uprightly in true and pure light. The sons then relay this information as the bread of the word of God so that the young and aspiring seeker can partake as due. There is a son of God to be found in every land. God has prepared, readied and planted them all over the earth so none is left out. The connection to the universal web of life is realized through the exercise of faith in God and obedience to words of Truth through Christ. The connection is telepathic in nature or by wireless communication and requires that the heart be pure to receive. The Holy Ghost carries the information within while the Holy Spirit powers this network of the divinely appointed.

Grace sustains the young believer and helps to establish him so that he can grow in faith to stand before God in mercy. Only the matured in faith can come into the realm of mercy where the best of God can be experienced. The faithful that has come into the realm of mercy is a son who can plead to God on behalf of other men. He can plead so that their petitions are received in good favor and their sins forgiven by the Heavenly Father. He is God's chosen through whom other men can have experience of the marvelous. Each faithful one that has been so-called must therefore be forgiving and have compassion for the spiritually ignorant. He must forgive so as to have access to the fullness of the riches realized within the Divine economy. Many will fail to perceive the sons of light due to spiritual blindness and treat them with derision for the blind are strangers to the Divine. The sons must forgive such for forgiveness is divine and compassion makes for the sublime.

The faithless in his self-conceited pride is a constant irritant that irks the spirit of the faithful and humble. The latter must always have compassion for their ignorance as they know not what they speak of or do. The faithful believer is called to lead the spiritually blind who are willing from under the bondage of self into the freedom of the selfless through Christ. In order that his joy may be full, the faithful must never cease from showing compassion and mercy for many do not yet know. He must always be a midwife that delivers from darkness into light. Goodness overcomes evil just as light chases away darkness. God has ordained much work for the fully matured in Christ. It is for such that they have been called and chosen. Many who profess to follow after Christ have not come into true knowledge yet and still live outside of the Divine will. They have been stuck in grace for long and are yet to be established in mercy so as to stand upright before God. The great challenge of the body of Christ is to wean many away from the alluring indolence of grace on to the vitality of mercy so that such may come into the deeper knowledge and fuller understanding of God.

Every faithful one that is connected to the universal web of life has been reborn in light. To be reborn in light bestows the full anointing of God and it is shared by all who have come into his Divine presence. To be bestowed with full divine anointing is to also have the mind of Christ which makes the believer to seek to please the Heavenly Father always. He who has been bestowed with the mind of Christ has become a chosen one that drinks from the river of life that is as pure as crystal. It is the water of this river that sustains the tree of life. The river is the stream of hidden knowledge and uncorrupted information that flows from the mind of God to extend to the branches of the tree of life. The tree of life is the family of the exalted in spirit that have been adopted into the family of God. The branches of the tree of life are the anointed in full light that live to serve God's will. All such are family members of the household of God and are given to realize the kingdom of God on earth. All who are hooked up to the pure stream of knowledge and divine wisdom do become re-creators who bring out things that are new out of the old. Such do become the channels for things divinely inspired as the wellsprings of regeneration. In contrast, the unworthy and faithless do come to live under the overwhelming stream of corrupted information that flows from the tree of the knowledge of good and evil. The hearts of all that feed from the tree of knowledge and evil soon become pits of degeneracy and junkyards for the expendable things of the world.

The dynamo of the kingdom of God (in heaven) operates on the three components of the Father, the Son and the Holy Ghost. The Father communicates with the 'sons' through the medium of the Holy Ghost. It is a relationship much like capacitive sensing for the sons are the 'Lambs of sacrifice' acceptable and well-received by God. The love impulses, much like electricity, induced by the Father's touch on the 'lambskins' of his sons transfers the Divine healing power as well as knowledge and wisdom to them. It is this touch that imparts the sweet smelling fragrance of the offering well-received by God on to his sons. The spiritual charge and the fragrance confirm the touch of God. It confers divine power and enables the sons to walk under the cloak of divinity among men filled with knowledge and wisdom.

The dynamo of the kingdom of God (on earth) operates on the three components of water, blood and the spirit. The sons bring the living water of life from above through the word of Truth to those that seek. The believers who drink the living water of the words of life and live by it are the lifeblood of the kingdom. Obedience to Truth makes divine power to course through the believer. True and sincere belief constitutes the blood. The water relates with the blood through the medium of the Holy Spirit. It is the power of God in the words spoken by the sons and embraced by the believer that enables him with the power to carry out God's wishes. It is more like an inductive effect. Put more simply, the Father in heaven makes the sons to be aware of his will through the Holy Ghost. The sons of God embody the connection between Heaven and earth. The sons convey the will of the Heavenly Father to the believers on earth. The believers on earth are induced by the Holy Spirit or the power in the words received to carry out God's will on earth.

Each son is a vessel chosen and kept apart by God to serve him with due honor and glory. He is called to carry out his 'divine charge' with diligent prudence for he has been equipped with the wings of strong faith that lifts mankind to the exalted heights where the dew of the latter rain can be soaked up. The latter rain brings the best saved for last for humanity by God at a time when many will be hungering for new. Each son is timely appointed to bring healing and new life into the human experience by inducing the willing on to the path of righteousness where the new is realized through Christ. But such must remain on guard and watch out always for the forces of darkness that aim to prevent many from having a taste of new life by disobedience to Truth. But every son has been well equipped to overcome such opposition through Christ. It is a seal of faith and inscription of honor that marks the sons.

- ✓ The malcontent in spirit will never know peace within as well as the goodness of God.
- ✓ The truly noble spirit is selfless and thankful to God for life's gifts.
- ✓ The faithful led on the righteous path will always hear the reassuring and comforting words of God.
- ✓ The image of Christ is that of the heavenly manifested in the earthly in loving light.
- ✓ The mind that is not cluttered with the worldly has left ample room for the spiritual to abound.
- ✓ The connection to the web of life is realized by the exercise of faith and obedience to words of Truth.
- ✓ The pride and self-conceit that fill the faithless irk the spirit of the faithful believer.
- ✓ The faithful that lives by Truth will be divinely immunized and protected from all his troubles.
- ✓ The river of life is the stream of hidden knowledge that flows from God's heavenly throne to earth.
- ✓ The touch of the Divine imparts a sweet smelling fragrance on the faithful in the way.
- ✓ Power to overcome evil is the seal of approval and mark of honor of the faithful in Christ.

Heart that confesses in love

With spirit purified in Truth

Is a temple of true worship

And a divine dwelling place

Chapter 19

AN ORDAINED PURPOSE

When clearly understood, the words of the Holy Scriptures embody eternal Truth or that which will always remain true. The faithful believer that receives such Truth into his heart in good faith will in due time be nurtured to full spiritual maturity and into a better understanding of the important in life. Truth abides forever, never passes away and contains the essence of the Divine which is life. Therefore he in whom the word of God has taken root to abound and be established will never pass away for his soul will always abide. The mind of such a believer will reflect that of Christ and operate in union with the Divine to serve the sovereign will. The spirit within such a believer will forever exist for he is joined up inseparably with the everlasting. Such a believer has conquered death to become like a tree planted beside the still waters whose leaves remain ever verdant. It takes such leaves nourished by the light of Truth to sustain both the tree as well as all those willing to receive with nuggets of wisdom in love.

The faithful believer that has matured in this light is one that is given to speak about things glimpsed from behind the veil of Heaven. He is given to speak such words that come from the throne of the Heavenly Father to bring healing to receiving hearts. The latter are those who have chosen the way of Christ which leads to life and rejected worldliness which leads to death. Where Truth is well received, the receiver will come to awaken in a spirit of new life. He will be led to the Divine in due course with Heaven's approval. Such is the power to do the marvelous in the words spoken when the heart is pure and the believer is deemed righteous by God. The righteous before God have been planted all over the world. The days of their manifestation have already begun as they labor in the spirit of the Divine to effect transformational changes all over the world. They labor not for themselves but for humanity as led by the Divine. They labor not for gain or fame but for God's approval and love. Their lines reach up to Heaven and their branches have gone all over the world for theirs is a universal web of life that derives its consciousness and motivation from God's throne.

Mankind has come into the season of harvest. The planting of the seed of God's word has been completed all over the world. In many places and in many hearts the words have failed to take deep root and have even shriveled to become fruitless. But in other places and within certain hearts, the words have become anchored in deep roots to grow into full maturity and produce fruit.

Such hearts that have produced desired fruits to God's glory are called to remain ever ready to serve faithfully so that they can produce even more fruits. Such that are righteous before him may face many trials but are sustained by God's love to overcome their troubles and to pollinate others with the divine essence as due.

Every righteous one is of the 'Lazarus' generation and are counted with those who have died and risen with Christ. They have each become spiritually transformed to the divine image and have become a place of habitation for God on earth. The process of transformation begins when the spirit within becomes humble and sincere to embrace Truth. Embracing 'the seed of Truth' faithfully results in a spiritual pregnancy. The pregnancy has to be nourished through faithful obedience to God's commands in order to come to full term. The outcome of this process is the spiritual man of Christ that steps forth through Divine power to replace the old self. The 'Christ-Man' is born or steps forth from within when he has come to full spiritual maturity in the way and not when he is conceived. It takes at least seventeen years for the 'Christ-Man' to come to full spiritual maturity from conception. Every 'Christ-Man' is a son of God who is able to know all things for the Heavenly Father will not hide anything when such earnestly seek.

The fully matured new man within is a son of God who is equipped to harness Divine power to do the amazing before mankind. In these days, each son has an array of tools to help his endeavors and is linked with other sons in spirit within the divine commonwealth. The latter is a congregation of the spirits of just men being 'perfected' in Christ. This congregation is a spiritual beehive that pulsates with the divine consciousness of the living church. All congregants of this living church without walls work towards the common goal of establishing the heavenly way on earth. Though sundered far and wide all over the world, by faith they do indeed meet around the mercy seat of the Almighty God. Although it may not appear that way to the spiritually blind, God's grand purpose of changing the earth into Heaven is steadily and surely taking place through such that have matured in spirit through Christ. This change is taking place even as the present age steadily passes away. These are the last days of the present world order for a new one is unfolding. The latter is the golden age of mankind and it is about to dawn as those in union with the Divine already know.

There are clues woven into the fabric of the words of scriptures that are increasingly being revealed to the faithful as mankind comes to the close of this age. These embody the meat of Truth that only the mature in Christ are able to eat and digest. The fullness of the riches of God can never be attained until Christ has come to full maturity within the believer. Mankind will never know in full until he is born as a 'Christ-Man' and not when he is conceived. From the eater of the bread of the word of God comes out the meat of the Spirit in its due season. The faithful believer that is filled with the meat of the Spirit can understand hidden Truth and mysteries of God's kingdom. These mysteries constitute the hidden knowledge by which the natural is transformed to the spiritual and the earthly changed to the heavenly. It has remained the same from the foundation of time and will be for all ages to come. Out of the mouth of God were all things created and out of the mouths of the righteous that stand before him will the same continue. Such have the power to re-create or change much in the present world through their spoken words in accordance with God's divine will.

The fully transformed have come into the spiritual fellowship between the Heavenly Father and his sons. This is the realm of the eternal where the tree of life stands. It is the new Eden where the provident will of God is showcased as he communes in spirit with the righteous. Within this realm reserved only for the fruitful, lies the knowledge of those things upon which Heaven and earth are founded. Only by walking in this garden appointed only for noble souls is mankind able to attain true fulfillment in life. Fulfillment does not come through the material but through the spiritual. It can only come by knowledge borne of assurance that one has been included in the book of life through spiritual experiences and communion with the Divine. It is in the realm of fruitful trees that God is given to work things out for the righteous before him. Thereabouts is found the wisdom that hopes for all things good. Thereabouts is where pertinent knowledge is received so that the righteous can always build on a solid foundation. Thereabouts are the true and pure made known so that the righteous can remain a true shining beacon that draws other men to the heavenly way.

The impurities of the world have to be cleaned from his soul before mankind is able to be 'magnetized' and spiritually drawn to the Heavenly Father. Once magnetized in this way, the purified soul can in turn magnetize and draw others unto God. The magnetizing force is the love of God expressed through the spirit essence in the words of Truth. It works to draw all who embrace Truth back to God from whom all things came forth in the first place. All such are being drawn back to the home that they once knew. All who will come to know the Divine in the way of Christ were pre-known by the Heavenly Father. All such are kindred spirits borne of a source that remains unchanging and are known to each other from the foundation of time.

Chapter Notes

- ✓ Words of Truth abide forever wherever such has been embraced and well received.
- ✓ The reborn are linked together in a web of life that derives its consciousness and motivation from God.
- ✓ The cultivation of the seeds of Truth has been completed and mankind is in the season of harvest.
- ✓ The faithful transformed into the spiritual image of Christ have become the dwelling place of God.
- ✓ The congregation of the justified is a 'beehive' that pulsates with the impetus of the Divine.
- ✓ The fullness of the riches of God is afforded to the faithful that has come into full spiritual maturity.
- ✓ Fullness of joy is not attained by the material but by living in the provident will of God.
- ✓ The love of God expressed by the words of Truth works to magnetize willing hearts to the Divine.
- ✓ Fulfillment is found at the convergence of the heavenly and earthly where man finds purpose.

Wisdom gives much in light

The faithful able to receive

Is called to share with all

And sow in labors of love

Chapter 20

BOND OF LOVE

The way of Christ is to live in the light of Truth and to have compassionate love for all. The power in the blood of the lamb of sacrifice only works for those who love Truth and live thereby in love. Only those who speak in Truth are able to hear the inaudible voice of the Divine spirit who speaks through Christ. In as much as love is the bond that holds the body of Christ together, Truth is the means by which love communicates. It is either yes or no and dos or don'ts within the divine fold. It takes Truth to set the believer free in spirit and give him strength within to endure the walk on the righteous path. It takes Truth blended with the blood of sacrifice of the 'lamb of God' to avail the power to bind the enemy, free the spirit and make the amazing happen in life. Truth that is blended with sacrificial love is the anti-dote to the darkness in the world and the impetus for the spread of light.

It is only through noble sacrifices made in truth that the sinful nature within mankind can be laid to rest. The power in the sacrificial blood of Christ shows forth in him who has rejected the disingenuous ways of the world to embrace Truth. It demands courage to embrace the message of Truth through Christ for there is a stiff price to pay for not living as most in the world do. Initially the decision to choose God's way will be very costly for the aspiring seeker but will prove to be worthwhile in the end. In time the hatred and derision of the world do turn to love and praise for the man transformed through Christ. The seeker will endure mockery but he will receive blessings later. Therefore he must be willing to lose everything if so called but he will gain back all that is needful in due season. The road upwards is steep and the journey long but the reward is truly 'out of this world'. It is okay to pay the toll of thirty pieces of silver that the world demands of the faithful so that he can pass from the earthly on to the heavenly.

Humanity has passed the pivotal crossroads and come into the season of self-examination. Everyone must be certain of the choice that he has made for the harvest season is upon humanity. Mankind is on the verge of the end of grace where the bridegroom steps away. It is about time for the children of the bride chamber to begin to fast. It is a season for the established in faith through grace to stand and be counted in mercy. The baby who has been held up by others so as to learn how must now walk by himself. The lame man who has been rehabilitated to stand must now walk. The blind whose sight has been restored has to perceive the better so that he can no longer be deceived.

It is the season for the freed in spirit to soar to the exalted realm so as to abound in good works and bear faithful witness about the goodness of God to mankind.

Even as unsaved man wonders in confused dissolution as to where the world is headed, the redeemed in Christ already know this to be the season of hope and renewal for God's chosen. The wheat is being separated from the tares and the saved from the unsaved. It is eventide in humanity's day and only the worthy before God can make it through the night. There is a choice that urgently begs to be made by mankind. It is a choice between Christ and the world. It is a choice between life and death. It is a choice of citizenship in the new heaven on earth or spiritual death. This is the time to enter while there is still room. The Heavenly Father has prepared enough sons all over the world to guide true seekers into divine light as the last responders to humanity's cry to God for help.

The faithful that has cast his lot with God must maintain his worthiness by keeping the lamp of Truth burning brightly in his heart. He that has sacrificed all for love and Truth to attain the priceless must safeguard his prize. He has obtained that which is eternal and can never be taken away. He is now joined to the hub of creation and can fashion things that are new out of the old. Such that are so joined are given to do the things that are praise worthy, lovely and of a good report. He must remain willing to pay the price for loving Christ as he finishes his course in the earthly plane. The heart that does not love Truth and therefore is without Christ hates those who live by Truth. Even though the faithful in Christ speaks the Truth in blessing he must always make accommodation for the hatred of the world. He must have compassion and hold out hope for the ignorant who continue to reject Truth.

Most men live by the shadow of Truth and not by it. They live in accordance with what is commonly acceptable and what they can get away with it. Such live by compromise of Truth. They do not live to please God who they cannot see with the eyes of the flesh. Rather they live to please and win the favors of other men. They presume to know it all but little do the wise in their own eyes know. The Heavenly Father is not a God of shadows but of Light. As a matter of fact, he is the Light that nothing can hide from. Therefore the faithful in Christ constantly watches and prays for wisdom in order not to be marred with the tar of the world. Although the world hates those who live by Truth, the faithful in the way need not worry for he abides under the wings of the Almighty Father. The contenders for the glory of the world may have their fleeting moments but the glory of the world does not endure. The faithful in light will yet remain victorious for the unseen hand of the Father fights his battles for him.

The faithful that lives in the light of Truth and love is dearly beloved by God for such is the little one whom his Father cannot help but love. It is through the beloved that the wisdom and power of God is showcased for mankind to witness. God's countenance always shines on the beloved and his eyes rest upon them. It is when such that are beloved feels most vulnerable and at the weakest that the strength and power of God shows forth to aid them. It is in those moments that the warmth of the Father's boundless love and tender mercies are known. It is at the weakest moments that the faithful in the way must learn to listen for he will hear love's inaudible voice of comfort. It is in the most miserable times that he must keep hope alive. It is in the darkest hours that he must hold on. The dark seasons of life repeat, just as night follows day, to teach man that he really is a little dear one before God. The dark season of life is when the faithful learns to trust the all-knowing Father who never fails to bring light and life to the hopeful. It is during the dark periods that life's clutters are sorted out and those things that are not needed are discarded. It is during the dark periods that the tutoring still small voice of Hope teaches the faithful to ask for that which he desires for the Father will not deny him who has kept faith.

It is essential that those faithful in the way learn to hope and wish for those things that are true, honest, pure, just, lovely and virtuous. Those are ingredients that make up things that are praise worthy and of a good report before God. The faithful must keep the words of Truth hidden and burning brightly in the heart so that the eye of the spirit is not beclouded by the noise and smoke of the world which works to dim the soul. The things that one thinks about are the things that will come to take shape in his life. The faithful that lives in accordance with Truth in the spirit of Christ will think kingly thoughts and take princely steps. Such will be connected to the Divine to overcome all and triumph in life.

The mind that is joined with the Divine is uncluttered and has ample room for things that pertain to godliness. Worldly possessions can clutter the mind and cloud the soul if due care is not taken. In the absence of cloudiness, there is a definite certainty and clarity of purpose infused into the spirit within. Certainty of spirit and clarity of purpose help define the glorious dawn. He that is joined in spirit with the Divine is given to recreate the heavenly on earth as a domain of light in which darkness ceases to exist. The glorious dawn has no ebb and therefore no night time. It is in the glorious dawn that orderliness returns to life, confusion recedes and focus is sharpened. The faithful that awakes in a glorious dawn is no longer carried about by the opinion of others that turn out to be clouds without rain but is able to ascertain the true and pure in Christ.

Chapter Notes

- ✓ Truth blended with goodness is the impetus for light and the anti-dote to darkness.
- ✓ It takes the goodness in the blood of Christ to cancel out the evil in the blood of the sinful.
- ✓ Mankind has arrived at the pivotal crossroads where everyone has to be certain in his choice.
- ✓ As the world wonders where all is headed, the redeemed know this as the season of good hope.
- ✓ Even though Truth is spoken in blessing, the rejection of a disbelieving world remains a given.
- ✓ The unfaithful is soon led to become an agent of darkness that will never know the Divine.
- ✓ The reborn may be little in the eyes of the world but he is loved beyond all measure by Heaven.
- ✓ Duty calls the faithful to desire only such that are lovely and worthy of praise from God.
- ✓ Certainty and clarity of purpose is infused into life when the spirit within is free of worldly cares.
- ✓ Night time ceases to exist when the heart becomes lit with the flame of love.

Eternity becomes final destination

When man's footsteps are after God

Such will come into realm of delights

And join the everlasting song of joy

Chapter 21

STARS OF HEAVEN

The act of mercy is an immensely useful and productive spiritual asset in the portfolio of the follower after Christ. Mercy works in a paradoxical way, for it abounds when tendered and shrinks when withheld. The realm of mercy is a place very close to the Divine heart. It is the preserve of those who have proven worthy in Christ to become known by God. It is the spiritual realm of the sons of God whose wishes the Father delights to grant. To grow into full maturity in light through Christ subjects the faithful to much suffering and hurt at the hands of the worldly. The believer will suffer not only at the hands of unbelieving strangers but also family, friends and acquaintances. The faithful believer is often taken advantage of, put to ridicule, blatantly lied against, wrongfully accused and mostly misjudged.

Such a faithful one is called to endure and persevere through his heartaches and pains. It is the only way for the ego of the flesh to be decreased so that the inner man of the spirit can increase. It is all very hurtful for the seeker but it is in fact necessary because the flesh does not yield easily to the spirit. All the injustices heaped upon the faithful believer add up to the process of crucifixion by which the old self is buried so that the new man of the spirit can be realized. For man to begin to ascend in spirit, he must pass through the figurative eye of the needle. The latter separates the heavenly from the earthly. It takes crucifixion to streamline mind, body and spirit so as to be able to pass through the eye of the needle for ascension to the exalted heights.

The faithful that is able to ascend in spirit has come to the heavenly side of the cross. The benefits found there far outweigh the agony of crucifixion. He that has come to the heavenly side must learn to be merciful to all who wrong and grieve him. It is the only way that he can be able to share and abound in the Hope that he has found for the tender mercies of God will follow him everywhere. The treasure trove of mercy is immense and exhaustless. The tender mercies are promised, received and enjoyed through forgiving love. There is no recrimination or bitterness mixed in with mercy. The sunshine of divine love always shines in mercy with joyful exuberance and cannot wait for the dawn of each morning. It cannot wait for the birds to chirp. It cannot wait for the flower to unfold. The sunshine of love cannot wait to hear the sweet melody of life playing once again. Every son of God is borne in love and is a 'sun' of righteousness. Therefore each son must strive to keep the flame of divine love alive in his heart by forgetting the hurt rendered to him by all for that is the essence of mercy and the good life.

In order to come into the full anointing of God, the faithful believer must do away with the needless things that clutter his life. He must simplify and arrange his priorities in life so that orderliness can be established. Doing so allows for the focus to be put on the things that will prove to be lovely and of a good report. This re-arrangement or pruning of his life allows the faithful believer to find the core of his true self. It is this core that responds readily to Truth. The faithful believer has to go through this pruning alone within a sort of wilderness in life. It is in this season when he is seemingly alone and forsaken by many that he is able to understand the true essence of the Divine. It is in this season that the believer comes to know fully and to begin to see in the clarity of the higher and purer. This is when he will begin to live life fully as Christ reborn and less in conformity with the world for he has entered where the flesh profits nothing but the spirit profits everything.

When the faithful ceases to live in conformity with the world, he will enter into a commencement of true confession. His words will become few and measured. He will only speak the much needed to bear testimony about Truth. It has to be so for his heart has become the wellspring of life out of which flows living water. He has become a man of certainty who will not compromise his faith and so must guard his tongue. Such that has become a fountain of life must strive to remain righteous for God now commands his obedience in all things and at all times.

He that has yielded his will to God has escaped from the domain of shadows into the realm of light where confusion abates and serenity reigns over the soul. God's grace has enabled him to scale the ladder of faith through Christ. He has been lifted into the realm of mercy to become one able to overcome and garner victory over the enemy. Many who strive to come into the realm of mercy fail on account of love for the material things of the world. In loving the world to a fault, they leave little room in themselves to be filled with the requisite measure of the essence of godliness needed to overcome the world. Therefore they remain bound to the world as sons of men and are not able to escape its shackles as sons of God.

The faithful believer that has been lifted in spirit into the realm of mercy is soon revealed to all who are perceptive by the Heavenly Father. He that has buried the flesh of his old self and forsaken the world for love of God through Christ comes to be duly acknowledged in due season. This acknowledgement comes in form of the ability to receive information and knowledge flashed into the mind through the Holy Ghost. He will become tuned in spirit to the inaudible voice of the Holy Ghost that brings affirming and comforting thoughts from the mind of the Father above to his sons below. He that has been lifted into the realm of mercy will know what to pray for and when to pray for it for he has entered the season of the refreshing of the latter rain. Such will cease to labor in his own flesh but be enabled rather by the spirit of God in his endeavors. He will face many temptations and fight many spiritual battles. But to his advantage, he will always have fore knowledge through the Holy Ghost to help prepare him for victory through his troubles.

The faithful one tuned in spirit to the Holy Ghost can battle and defeat the enemy because he will always have informed and insightful knowledge in all situations. Most believers perish at the hands of the enemy for lack of informed knowledge about what is going on around them in life. The Holy Ghost provides that hidden and inside knowledge that most who profess to follow Christ do not have access to. By extension, the believer tuned in spirit to hear the Holy Ghost becomes the bearer of light in a dark world. Such have been prepared and stationed as lighthouses all over the world to guide those given to embrace Truth through the storms of life into safe harbor. Each son is a giant of faith who has been given the Holy Ghost to inform him about things and the Holy Spirit to help him make things happen. The Holy Ghost is the ample brain and the Holy Spirit ample brawn that embody the spiritual giant or Colossus of faith.

Each spiritual giant (as a son of God) has the potential to do all things and can initiate the trend of things on earth.

He is assigned an earthly plot and handed the script of life. The script of life frames the battle of good against evil and light over darkness. The earthly plot is a drama stage that depicts life on which character actors are called to play certain roles in good faith. Their roles have already been ordained by the Heavenly Father. All will be judged on how well they perform their roles for there is an award at the end. Each son is like a director that guides others on how to give laudable performances that will please God on life's grand stage. The Heavenly Father is the executive producer but he has anointed each son to be a director of events on the earthly lot ordained for him. Each son must always have the right script by having his mind focused on the heavenly so that he can turn out a winning production as expected of him. He must direct every stage production so that good defeats evil and light triumphs over darkness as should. To do otherwise is to engage in an unwinnable fight with Omnipotence. To veer off the assigned script is an attempt to upset the apple cart of Heaven.

Chapter Notes

- ✓ Mercy is a useful and productive spiritual tool in the treasure chest of the matured in light.
- ✓ Love learns to forgive the injustice and injuries suffered at the hands of others.
- ✓ There must be no recrimination so that the promises of love can be duly received and enjoyed.
- ✓ The faithful that puts his life in good order is able to put focus on the things that matter with God.
- ✓ The tongue that speaks in testimony to Truth must be well-guarded and speak only measured words.
- ✓ The faithful that yields to the Divine will escape from darkness to have serenity reign over the soul.
- ✓ Each son is acknowledged and revealed by God to all who are perceptive in spirit in due season.
- ✓ Victory over the enemy is availed by informed and insightful knowledge about the important in life.
- ✓ God assigns a plot to be cultivated into a garden of fruitful trees to every faithful believer.

The long running drama of life below

Is a motion picture for those above

Tis apples of gold turned in due time

'to pictures of silver to be seen by all

Chapter 22

THE WALK OF FAME

The star lit night is the silver screen and canvas that reflects the earthly handiworks of the sons of God in twinkling majesty. Each son is a golden award director whose masterful work is held up in immortal display for mere mortals to gaze at. The glory of God shed on his sons leave mere mortals star-struck for their works do indeed shine brilliantly before mankind. Everyone that is willing to embrace Truth is cast for a role in the grand performance of life. There are different roles and parts to play in life's drama but it is divinely assigned through pre-destination. All whose eyes have been opened to understand this must perform their roles with brilliant honor. The role performed with brilliant honor is the life lived in faith and Truth in the service of goodness to humanity. The audience is the heavenly host that watches, judges and records all the earthly performances of mankind.

The faithful who have passed judgment before God are deemed worthy to be exalted to the starry heights. Such are deemed worthy to join the troupe of celestial stars who perform in endless majesty on the ultra-grand stage of the night sky. Every faithful one who has been well received by God has been planted to shine in light as a star of heaven. Each star must have some satellite planets that revolve around them for every son must bear offspring in the way of light. The satellite planets are those believers who have embraced Truth to come into knowledge of the Divine through the sons. The satellites are the wise virgins who fill their lamps with oil and wait patiently for the bridegroom in order to become 'married' to him.

The believers 'married' to the sons through faith are like plants in the garden given to be pollinated by the tree of righteousness in their midst. The tree of righteousness is that which stands when other trees are long gone. Some trees have been cut down and used for firewood. Others were struck by lightning and split apart. Some could not survive the strong winds and were blown down. Some could not survive the season of drought because they craved for much. Others were washed away in the season of the floods. Yet others could not survive the scourge of marauding and myriad infestations. The tree of righteousness is the lone tree that stands through all that felled others. It withstands the fire that burns the grass that clutters the land. The grass is that which seeks and lives for the praise of men. But the tree of righteousness is he that bears testimony to the power and faithfulness of God as he watches over the beloved flock. Each son of God is a tree of righteousness called to pollinate the plants that God has placed in his earthly lot for such will grow to full maturity and produce good fruits in their appointed seasons. Such is the reasonable service and laudable performance that translates the earthly into the heavenly as well as transform the mortal into immortality.

The book of life is the index of credits that lists the names of those who have performed their roles on earth with honor to Heaven's acclaim. Each son is a guiding light that illuminates the way so that the spiritually blind may find the way back to the Heavenly Father. Such is a member of the living church that is the congregation of Christ. He lives to bring men closer to the knowledge of God by translating the heavenly ways on earth. The anointing of Christ is bestowed on the sons so that they can untie the knots of spiritual bondage, lift the veil of spiritual blindness, obtain forgiveness for the sinful and resuscitate the moribund among mankind. It is the same anointing yesterday, today and forever given to make the dead in spirit to live again in the light of Truth in love. It is the same Truth shared and well taken to heart that make sons of God out of mortal men. It is the same redeeming light that shines brilliantly into the dark recesses of hearts to chase away the fears and torments of darkness forever.

Each son of heaven belongs to the vanguard of greater enlightenment divinely chosen to bring a deeper and better understanding of the heavenly ways to blind humanity. Each is an illuminator that helps to highlight and process the meat of spiritual Truth for clearer and better understanding. Each son is a man of strong faith and courage who can be entrusted with due new knowledge by the Father. By them do men come into the knowledge of new things that flow from the heavenly throne. They are such that speak with certain knowledge for they have known God's unfailing faithfulness. The knowledge that they have is conveyed by the Holy Ghost and the assurance that they possess is affirmed by the Holy Spirit. He that has both the Holy Ghost and the Holy Spirit is an oracle of the Divine that speaks with truthful courage. The oracle is the voice of divine reasoning that seeks to guide mankind back on to the path of righteousness. The oracle does not use his gift for personal gain but to tend the sheep of God's flock. The oracle speaks to specific situations and clamors not for the artificial light of the world stage but lives in hope for a starring role in the immortalized silver screen up above.

Each son is connected with the Heavenly Father and with the other sons in a web pulsing with life and knowledge. What one son knows the others can know and what one has the others can have too. It is a spiritual commonwealth in which the sons are connected in love. They do not seek for an audience to show what they know for they seek not the praise of men. Rather each son labors to use what he has been entrusted with to bring others into the marvelous light of God through Christ. Such is not overwhelmed by the flood of information that abounds in today's world. He is shielded from the surreptitious and wasteful but guided to that which is needful. He is anchored on solid rock and therefore the overwhelming floods of the present cannot overtake him. He knows the right choices to make, the right answers to give and the right path to walk in life. He is one that always strives to appropriate and use what he has been given to serve God's divine purposes on earth.

Each son must always give a wonderful performance in order to please the eager eyes of the Heavenly Father who watches from his throne above. In order to do so, he must always keep the unclean spirit at bay. The latter is the viral and corrupting impulses that seek to pull him back into that past which he has escaped from. It aims to lead him back with seductive and gentle persistence into the slippery domain of shadows where darkness is not far removed. It seeks to beguile him into life's basement where the decrepit soul makes his home. Each son must be on guard for the unequal yoking that infringes upon his 'life' in God. He must let the dead bury the dead. He has been chosen and kept apart by God. In order to remain so, he will displease many in the short term but in the long term all will thank God for him.

The unclean spirit is a devourer and feasts in the hearts of those who profess Christ but have not partaken worthily of grace. Such heard the message but did not heed faithfully

They picked and chose what to obey or not obey. They performed their undertakings always with an eye for the praise of men and personal gain. The unclean spirit is the spirit of instability and contending opposites that steadily tears apart the soul of its host. Such a host may appear to be okay one day but is deeply troubled the next. It can be likened to a bipolar existence where the host has built his house on shifting sand instead of the solid rock of God through Christ. The unclean spirit aims to chip away at the foundation of faith. It is much like a virus that strikes stealthily to misdirect and confuse the infirm in spirit. Truth is the firewall that protects from the intrusion of the unclean destabilizing spirit. Truth affords passage through the valley of the shadow of death so that the enemy may chase but never catch up to those sanctified by it. If and when the enemy catches up with any sanctified in Truth such will be powerless to do him harm for he has become immune to evil. All who are immune to evil are the overcomers that can indeed do the marvelous in life by faith through Christ. Such are the new vessels and their content the divine new wine.

Chapter Notes

- ✓ Divine glory shed on mankind make for works that shine brilliantly to leave mortals star struck.
- ✓ Each son is a tree of righteousness divinely planted to pollinate those that are planted in his lot.
- ✓ The book of life is the index of credits that lists the names that have performed honorably on earth.
- ✓ The reborn have been chosen to bring a deeper and better understanding of the heavenly way.
- ✓ The believer in communion with the Divine makes right choices and walks on the right path in life.
- ✓ Worldliness constitutes the viral and corrupting that seek to pull the believer back into an ugly past.
- ✓ The unclean spirit feasts in the hearts of those who profess Christ but do not partake worthily of grace.
- ✓ Truth affords divine immunity to protect and give safe passage through the dark seasons of life.
- ✓ Truth is the firewall that protects from the unclean which makes the spirit within infirm.
- ✓ All who have divine immunity through Christ are given to do the marvelous in life.

Life is but the ultimate drama stage

Where each must play the right part

To frame the heavenly way on earth

So light can triumph over darkness

Books for Spiritual Guidance by Kalu Onwuka

Nuggets of Resurrection is an engaging discourse that explores the many gifts available to the spiritually matured in Christ, the path that seekers are called to walk as well as how to overcome challenges along the way.

Pulses of the Divine Heart is an uplifting and enriching study that attests to the abiding nature of God's love and the unfailing goodness of Providence to the faithful man whose spirit is in tune with the Divine.

Etching for the Heart is a timely, fascinating and insightful study that highlights the power of sacrificial love, good hope and the enlightenment of Christ to bring wholeness in the life of the faithful believer.

No Hurry to Horeb is a thoughtful discourse about how mankind can tune his inner awareness to rise above the lowliness of today's society and realize the fullness of life divinely appointed for those who truly aspire.

Echoes of the Golden thoughtfully and deeply explores the path that leads to spiritual transformation so that mankind can begin to see from a heavenly perspective and make the earthly experience much better.

Works of Poetry by Kalu Onwuka

Anthems in the Glorious Dawn is a rich collection of ninety-three poems to nourish the soul, uplift the spirit and help rekindle a relationship with God. The underlying message of the power of sacrificial love strikes a resonant chord.

In Enchantment of Eternity is a superb collection of ninety-four poems that touches the heart deeply through such topics as love, the benefits realized on life's high road as well as the vision and victory availed through strong faith.

Tones of the Stellar is a volume of eighty-eight inspirational poems that speaks to the freedom of spirit and wholeness of life availed by enlightenment through Christ. The remarkable verses offer timely guidance about reconnecting with God.

A Splendid Awakening is a simple yet eloquent collection of ninety-two inspirational poems that highlights how mankind must let go of his mistake-laden past to realize a fulfilling and enduring future full of God's blessing.

 *The Melody of Light* is a selection from the author's body of work that represents the very best of faith-based poetry. Brimming with insight and thoughtful lessons, the verses paint vivid images about the wholeness that love avails.

All titles are available as paperbacks or e-books and may be purchased through many retail outlets and on-line distribution channels including **amazon.com**. All titles may also be purchased through Granada Publishers at **www.granadapublishing.com** and excerpts of the author's work are available at **www.kaluonwuka.com**.

Kalu Onwuka is a prolific author who writes about faith-walk and the path to transformation within for better in this new age of spiritual awareness. A vanguard among the emerging breed of spiritual poets, he uses his works to highlight the path that mankind must walk in order to find a blissful balance between the earthly and the heavenly.

He is the author of *Ruminations on the Golden Strand* series which are in-depth studies based on spiritual and earthly experiences that frame modern living in a way to help mankind achieve the utmost within a relationship with the Divine. The series include *Nuggets of Resurrection, Pulses of the Divine Heart, Etching for the Heart, No Hurry to Horeb,* and *Echoes of the Golden.*

He is also the author of *Poems in Faithfulness to the Divine* series which are books of poetry and songs. These include *Anthems in the Glorious Dawn, In Enchantment of Eternity, Tones of the Stellar, A Splendid Awakening* and *The Melody of Light*. There are other works on the way including the forthcoming *Capsules of Divine Splendor.*

Onwuka is a teacher, poet, lyricist, electrical engineer and entrepreneur. He lives in California with his wife of many years with whom he has raised five children. As a follower of Christ Jesus as the Light of the world, he believes that all true spiritual paths eventually converge in Christ. He uses his writing to help many achieve spiritual transformation for a more fulfilling life.

www.ingramcontent.com/pod-product-compliance
Lightning Source LLC
Chambersburg PA
CBHW060150050426
42446CB00013B/2753